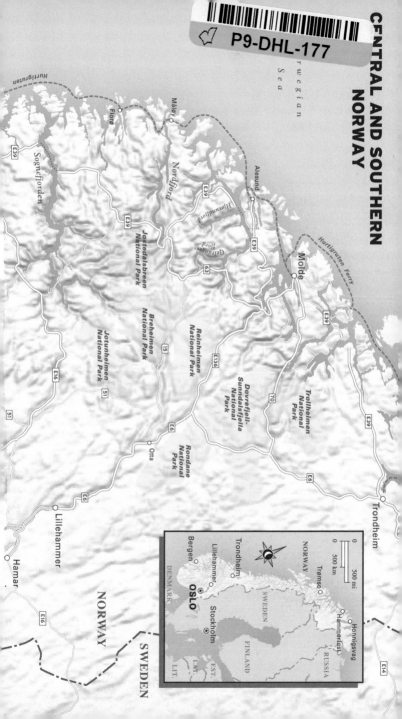

CENTRAL AND SOUTHERN NORWAY

P9-DHL-177

Norwegian Sea

Hurtigruten

Florø

Sognefjorden

Måloy

Nordfjord

Ålesund

Hjørundfjord

Jostedalsbreen National Park

E39

Geirangerfjord

63

Molde

Hurtigruten Ferry

Breheimen National Park

15

Reinheimen National Park

E136

Dovrefjell-Sunndalsfjella National Park

70

Trollheimen National Park

E39

Jotunheimen National Park

51

E6

Otta

Rondane National Park

E6

E16

E39

Trondheim

51

E6

Lillehammer

Hamar

NORWAY

E16

SWEDEN

NORWAY

SWEDEN

Bergen

Trondheim

Lillehammer

NORWAY

Tromso

Honningsvag

Hammerfest

OSLO

Stockholm

DENMARK

SWEDEN

FINLAND

RUSSIA

EST.

LAT.

LIT.

0   500 mi
0   500 km

E14

Contents

DISCOVER
Oslo

Oslo strikes a magical balance between history, modernity, and natural beauty.

Norway's cosmopolitan capital is a fast-growing city with an expanding list of arts, culture, and music events. The rejuvenated waterfront features a mix of old and new architecture, including the sparkling Oslo Opera House and the medieval Akershus Fortress.

Surrounded by water and forest, Oslo offers more outdoor experiences than any other city of its size. In the summer there is incredible hiking, biking, and boating, while in the winter you are never more than 20 minutes from a cross-country skiing trail. Beyond the capital city, historic Fredrikstad and sporty Lillehammer are both worthy of a day trip.

Come to Oslo and experience the magic for yourself.

Clockwise from top left: Vigeland Sculpture Park; modern buildings in Oslo; Akershus Fortress; Karl Johans gate; Oslo Opera House.

Planning Your Trip

When to Go

High season for tourism is June-August. This is the busiest time but also with the most diverse range of accommodations. July is the Norwegian holiday month, and bargains can be scored across Oslo.

A vastly underrated time is the spring. February-April, there is snow on the ground but the polar nights are long gone. Days are bright if crisp, and it's the best time for skiing. The weather in May is usually pleasant, but be aware of the many public holidays, most notably Constitution Day on May 17, when services for tourists are limited.

September-November is the rainy season. The dreary months of November-January are best avoided. Although the streets are brightened by festive lights, services for travelers are limited during the Christmas and New Year period.

Passports and Visas

Visitors entering the country are allowed to stay for up to 90 days.

Although Norway is not part of the European Union, it is a participant in the Schengen Agreement, which allows passport-free travel between member countries. If arriving from a fellow Schengen country (which includes most, but not all, EU members), there are no passport checks, but the 90-day period applies to the entire Schengen Area.

For citizens of the United States, Canada, United Kingdom, South Africa, New Zealand, and Australia and residents of the vast majority of European and Latin American countries, visas are not required to enter Norway at the time of writing.

Transportation

Most travelers arrive in Norway by plane, and almost all long-haul international flights into Norway arrive in Oslo.

Oslo is compact and easy to explore on foot. The city has an extensive public transit system, including metro, tram, bus, train, and ferry services, collectively managed under the umbrella organization Ruter. The Ruter network extends out of Oslo and into the surrounding Akershus county.

Oslofjord destinations such as Drøbak and Fredrikstad are easily accessible for day trips by car, bus, and/or train. Lillehammer is a little farther, a two-hour journey by car or train.

Best of Oslo

Twenty-first century Oslo is a city transformed. For decades, travelers would head straight for the mountains or the fjords, but today they linger in this cosmopolitan European capital with world-class architecture, art, and museums. Were it not for Norway's stunning natural environment, three days in Oslo would satisfy most travelers. That's because the city is intrinsically linked to nature, surrounded on all sides by forest and fjord. Spend an entire weekend break in Oslo or tag on this three-day itinerary to a longer tour and you will not leave disappointed.

Should the weather be good, consider replacing any of these choices with a day trip to **Drøbak,** a delightful fishing village on the Oslofjord, or to **Fredrikstad** to wander the streets of one of northern Europe's best-preserved fortified districts.

To conserve your budget, make the most of your hotel's breakfast buffet and plan to eat light for lunch. Many hotels offer the opportunity to compose a packed lunch from the breakfast buffet (for an additional charge), or just grab some fruit and snacks from a supermarket.

Day 1: Art and the Waterfront

A visit to the epic **National Gallery** affords the opportunity to see some of Edvard Munch's most famous works with none of the crowds you might expect. Take a leisurely lunch in one of the excellent waterside restaurants on the **Aker Brygge** wharf, or grab a quick bite from a coffee shop and head instead to the **Astrup Fearnley Museum of Modern Art** at the nearby Tjuvholmen development. In the afternoon, explore the buildings that inspired the castle in Disney's *Frozen* at **Akershus Fortress,** before completing your tour of the waterfront with a stroll on the roof of **Oslo Opera**

Astrup Fearnley Museum of Modern Art

Akershus Fortress

House. The nearby **Oslo Central Station** and **Jernbanetorget** square offer several options for dinner.

Day 2: The Great Outdoors

Oslo's excellent public transit brings forest and fjord within reach of all budgets. Take the metro to the **Frognerseteren** mountain lodge, where you can enjoy a slice of cake and a piping hot cup of cocoa before a walk through the forest to the world-class ski jump at **Holmenkollen.** On your way back to the city, stop off at Majorstuen and walk the short distance to take in the life's work of Gustav Vigeland at the remarkable **Vigeland Sculpture Park.** For an informal dinner head to the busy streets of **Grünerløkka,** where most restaurants turn into lively nightspots as the time ticks by.

Day 3: The Museums of Bygdøy

The Bygdøy peninsula is home to some of the country's best museums, clustered together amid the spacious homes of some of Oslo's wealthiest residents. The **Viking Ship Museum** displays restored ships found in burial mounds along the Oslofjord, together with tools and other objects that reveal much about the daily lives of the Vikings. Continuing the maritime theme, the **Kon-Tiki Museum** tells the fascinating tale of Thor Heyerdahl's Pacific expeditions through the original vessels and documentary films. Finally, watch actors bring an 18th-century farming community to life at the **Norwegian Museum of Cultural History,** a must-do during the summer. Splurge on dinner and drinks in the district of **Frogner,** which offers several high-end options.

Oslo

Look for ★ to find recommended sights, activities, dining, and lodging.

Highlights

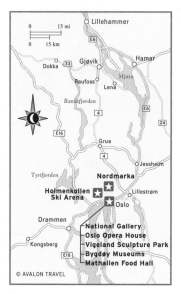

★ **National Gallery:** This impressive collection of artwork from across the ages rivals some of Europe's greatest galleries. The Edvard Munch room is a particular highlight (page 20).

★ **Oslo Opera House:** The award-winning architecture of this striking structure slopes gently into the Oslofjord. Walk up to the roof and take in the views from the top (page 22).

★ **Vigeland Sculpture Park:** Explore the life's work of Gustav Vigeland at the center of Frogner Park. Many of the 200 sculptures take human form (page 33).

★ **Bygdøy Museums:** Oslo's most interesting and unique cultural museums are gathered together on the Bygdøy peninsula. A day here is time well spent (page 34).

★ **Holmenkollen Ski Arena:** The views from the top of the ski jump at this world-class sporting arena are both breathtaking and stomach-churning (page 36).

★ **Nordmarka:** Packed with locals on weekends, the Nordmarka forest is the city's premier destination for hiking and cross-country skiing, less than a 30-minute metro ride from downtown (page 42).

★ **Mathallen Food Hall:** Some of the best restaurants in Oslo are gathered together under one roof (page 56).

Oslo is one of Europe's fastest growing cities and offers a growing list of cultural attractions to tempt the fjord-bound traveler to spend some extra days in the city. The combination of historic buildings, functional commercial districts, comfortable accommodations, and modern architecture attracts a diverse range of travelers to Norway's dynamic capital.

In recent years, Copenhagen and Stockholm have gotten into a very public battle for the rather meaningless marketing title "Capital of Scandinavia." Approach this subject in Oslo and locals will roll their eyes, safe in the knowledge that their city has become the modern cultural heartbeat of Scandinavia. After years of lying in the doldrums with a frankly deserved reputation of expensive dullness, Oslo's 21st-century renaissance has gathered pace in the blink of an eye.

First came the Aker Brygge fjord-side development of shops, restaurants, offices, and apartments replacing the unsightly Aker shipyard that greeted visitors arriving by sea. The motorway that further blighted the waterfront was ripped up and replaced with a network of tunnels. Oslo's waterfront is now a pleasant car-free environment, and it's set to improve even further.

With Oslo gaining in confidence as an emerging world city, attention turned to redevelopment of the east side. For several years since its opening in 2008, the sparkling white marble and glass Oslo Opera House stood alone as a symbol of the future, but development is finally underway on a new central library and Munch museum to complete the area's revitalization.

Almost all international travelers bound for the fjords will touch down

Oslo

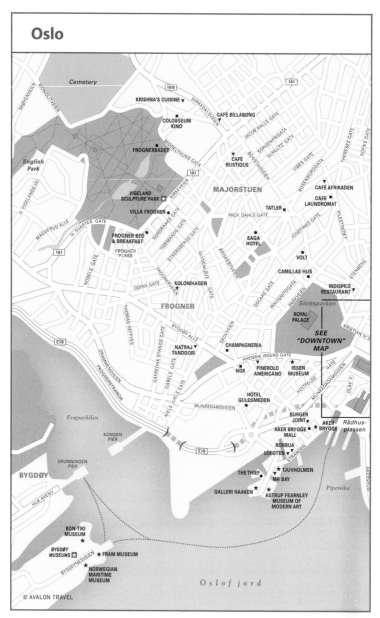

in Oslo, and finally the city has enough to demand attention and insist that all but the most nature-obsessed travelers should spend a day or two exploring the capital.

A city full of surprises to first-time visitors, Oslo is a much more cosmopolitan place than any other Norwegian city. One in three residents were

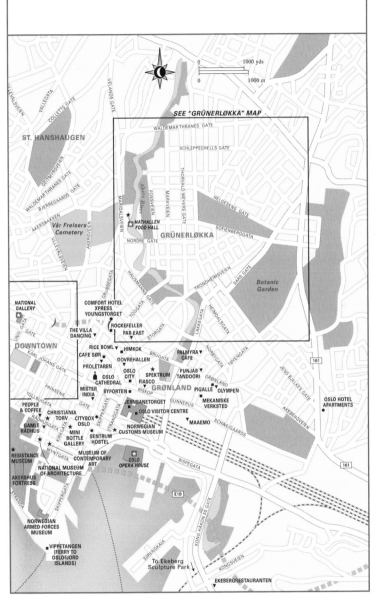

born outside of Norway, so mosques, temples, and a vast array of food and shopping options fill the city's streets.

Many visitors are surprised at Oslo's proximity to the great outdoors, offering more recreational opportunities than perhaps any other city of its size in the world. Despite a population of well under a million, the city is surrounded by water and forest, so in the summer there are awesome hiking, biking, and boating opportunities, while in the winter you are never more than a 20-minute metro ride from a cross-country ski trail.

Although it appears to be in the south of the country, Oslo is placed in the center of the region known as Eastern Norway thanks to the country's unusual geography. The region stretches along the Swedish border from the mountains south of Trondheim to the mouth of the Oslofjord. An extended stay in Oslo puts you within easy reach of great cities such as historic Fredrikstad or sporty Lillehammer, both worthy of a day trip if you'll be staying more than a couple days in Oslo.

HISTORY

Depending on your faith in ancient Norse sagas, King Harald Hardråde founded Oslo in 1049. There is evidence of earlier settlement, however, which puts Oslo at well over 1,000 years old. Either way, the original settlement stood at the foot of the Ekeberg hills to the east of today's central district.

The city's first golden age came way back in the Middle Ages. King Haakon V chose to live in Oslo at the beginning of the 14th century and build Akershus Fortress, two things that eventually led to the designation of Norway's capital switching from Bergen to Oslo.

This age of prosperity didn't last long. Like much of Europe, the city faced the horrors of the Black Death in 1349. A union with Denmark quickly followed, and the country remained in union with its Scandinavian neighbors (including Sweden at one point) until 1814. During this period, the development of Oslo slowed greatly and was largely overshadowed by the Hanseatic trading boom in Bergen.

In 1624 Oslo was destroyed by a three-day-long fire. King Christian IV declared that the old wooden city should not be rebuilt. Instead he built a new network of city streets behind Akershus Fortress. As was the king's prerogative, he named the new city Christiana. The old city continued to grow in an unmanaged state around its original location, populated with lower-class citizens.

Shipbuilding eventually pulled Christiana out of the doldrums, and the city's economy slowly began to stand on its own two feet. In the 19th century, Norway finally became an independent nation once again and formed a looser union with Sweden, and the city really took off. New institutions such as the University of Oslo and the National Gallery were opened, the city expanded along the Akerselva river and got its first railway. The Parliament building was constructed and the memory of Danish rule was slowly but surely wiped away. In 1877 the city name was changed to Kristiania, before the original Norwegian name of Oslo was restored in 1925.

Since the discovery of oil in the 1960s, Oslo, along with cities like Stavanger and Haugesund, has entered a boom era, attracting international investment and interest. But it wasn't until the political decisions of the late 20th century to redevelop so much of the waterfront that Oslo started the transition to in-demand tourist destination.

A little bit of Oslo changed forever with the terror attacks of July 2011, when a far-right extremist killed a total of 77 people, mostly children, in the city center and on nearby Utøya island. Then Prime Minister Jens Stoltenberg and the city's people responded to the atrocities with love and hope, a display of emotion and solidarity that gripped the world. An enormous bed of roses lay in front of the cathedral for weeks, and at a rallying event in front of the city hall a few weeks later, Stoltenberg proclaimed that "hope will win."

PLANNING YOUR TIME

Oslo offers something for you whether you have just an afternoon or an entire week. It would be remiss to visit Norway without spending at least a couple of days exploring the capital's unique attractions.

To take in the city's waterside attractions, visit the museums of Bygdøy, and explore at least some of the outdoor possibilities, allow three full days. Oslo is a surprisingly compact city and easy to explore on foot, but the excellent public transit system will speed things along if you're on a tight schedule.

For those spending a longer time in Oslo, it's worth considering some trips to nearby towns like Drøbak or Eidsvoll. A trip to Fredrikstad's beautiful Old Town is a great way to spend a summer's day, while Lillehammer is a must to rekindle memories of the 1994 Winter Olympic Games. Fredrikstad is just over an hour away by train or coach, and while Lillehammer is farther (more than two hours by car or train), it can be a comfortable day trip destination with some advance planning.

If your visit to Oslo is short, try to avoid Sunday and Monday. Almost all shops and some attractions are closed on Sunday, while many museums and galleries close on Monday. Opening hours are also restricted throughout the Norwegian holiday month of July.

Oslo Pass

If you stop by the modern **Oslo Visitor Centre** (Østbanehallen, Jernbanetorget, tel. 81 53 05 55, www.visitoslo.com, 9am-6pm daily), you will be offered the Oslo Pass. Available for 24, 48, or 72 hours, the pass gives you unlimited access on public transit; free parking in municipal car parks; free walking tours; entry to many museums, galleries, and attractions; and discounts in certain restaurants and stores. At 395kr (24 hours), 595kr (48 hours), or 745kr (72 hours), the pass isn't cheap. Note that children under 16 and seniors over 67 pay approximately half the adult rate, while students under 30 can claim a 20 percent discount with identification.

Whether the investment is worthwhile comes down to your traveling style and simple math. It's difficult to argue for the 24-hour pass unless you plan to rush around the city trying to cram as much as possible into one day. The 72-hour pass, however, is a different story. Consider the alternative:

There is no equivalent public transit pass, so you would need to buy a seven-day pass for 240kr. Visiting just four of Oslo's biggest attractions (National Gallery, Viking Ship Museum, the Norwegian Museum of Cultural History, and Holmenkollen Ski Museum) adds 435kr to your bill. At 620kr, the 72-hour pass can be a good value, especially if you visit even more places or take advantage of the discounts. Consider also the convenience factor of avoiding foreign currency transaction fees on your credit card or the accumulation of loose change.

The Oslo Pass can be bought at the Oslo Visitor Centre; Ruter public transit information centers at Jernbanetorget, Aker Brygge, or Oslo Airport; and from most museums and hotels. To obtain the child, senior, or student rate, you'll need to buy your pass at the Oslo Visitor Centre or from a Ruter center. You can also pre-order online and collect your pass at Oslo Visitor Centre. All passes come with a booklet listing the benefits and discounts available at each attraction.

ORIENTATION

The city of Oslo covers an area so large that a lake high up in the hills actually marks its geographic center. The sprawling forest surrounding the city on three sides is fiercely loved by locals and just as much a part of the city as the paved streets below. The forest is split broadly into **Nordmarka** to the north and **Østmarka** to the east, both accessible by public transit.

You'll spend most of your time in the compact **downtown** *(sentrum)* area. The few square miles of interest pivot around the main artery, **Karl Johans gate.** The mostly pedestrianized street slices straight through downtown Oslo, passing Oslo Cathedral, Parliament, and the National Theater on its way from Oslo Central Station to the Royal Palace. The city's **waterfront** is split into two bays; **Pipervika** to the west is home to the City Hall, Akershus Fortress, and Aker Brygge, while **Bjørvika** to the east is home to the Oslo Opera House, the gleaming office blocks and upscale restaurants of Barcode, and the luxury residential development Sørenga.

A short ferry trip into the **Oslofjord** reaches popular recreational islands. The pick of these is **Hovedøya,** with a nature reserve, important historical monuments, open space, and sheltered beaches.

Oslo's **suburbs** are divided by the Akerselva river. In simplistic terms, west of the river is more upmarket, with parks, expensive boutiques, and clean streets, while east of the river is more working class, with apartment blocks, cheaper shops and restaurants, and majority immigrant communities. Along the river itself is the hybrid **Grünerløkka,** a gentrified district full of boutiques, trendy cafés, and remarkable hairstyles.

Heading west, **Frogner** is an upper-class neighborhood great for shopping and home to most of the world's ambassadors to Norway. The important transit interchange at Majorstuen is a short distance from the sprawling Frogner Park and Vigeland Sculpture Park. Walking from downtown to Majorstuen via the Royal Palace and Frogner is a pleasant experience and great if you like shopping, thanks to the exclusive Bogstadveien shopping precinct.

Further to west is the peninsula of **Bygdøy,** of interest to travelers for the museums, as well as its beaches and hiking trails, which are popular with locals.

Immediately east of downtown, the diverse districts of **Grønland** and **Tøyen** offer the cheapest places to eat and shop in town but are short on sights. Farther east, Oslo's old town **Gamlebyen** doesn't compare to the historical districts of Fredrikstad, Bergen, Trondheim, and Stavanger, so there's no need to make a special journey.

Outside the central area, Oslo stretches for miles to the northeast and southeast with industrial and residential suburbs home to Oslo's rapidly increasing population.

Sights

Much of what you'll need to see in Oslo in located downtown, but don't miss the museums of Bygdøy, and take at least one trip into the hills.

All major museums and galleries have English explanations, either on the exhibits themselves or via a brochure. Where an establishment offers guided tours they are usually in Norwegian, with English available only on Saturday or by prior arrangement, often at a hefty cost. If a guided tour is important to you, inquire in advance.

DOWNTOWN

Oslo's compact center is packed with sights. You could pack in a day's sightseeing and have seen some of the world's most famous paintings and cultural experiences.

National Museum
(Nasjonalmuseet)

The **National Museum of Art, Architecture and Design** (tel. 21 98 20 00, www.nasjonalmuseet.no) is spread over a few distinct venues. The National Gallery, Museum of Contemporary Art, and the National Museum of Architecture are all worthy of a visit, especially as a combined ticket for all of the venues is just 100kr. All of the venues are closed on Monday. There is free entry on Thursday with extended opening hours until 7pm.

A new National Museum between the City Hall and Aker Brygge, scheduled to open in 2020, will combine all the museums together for the first time. As that time draws near, some of the exhibitions are likely to be reduced in size as the museums get ready for a logistical nightmare, so do check the latest status in advance if you're planning a special visit. The **Museum of Decorative Arts and Design (Kunstindustrimuseet)** (St. Olavs gate 1) is now closed pending the move.

Downtown Oslo

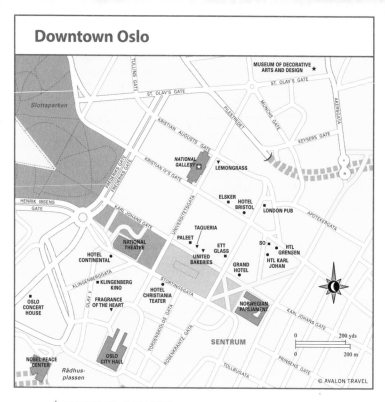

★ **NATIONAL GALLERY**
(Nasjonalgalleriet)

The city's star attraction is the vast **National Gallery** (Universitetsgata 13, 11am-6pm Tues.-Fri., 11am-5pm Sat.-Sun., 100kr). You could easily spend an entire day exploring Norway's largest public collection of paintings and sculptures, or just an hour if you want the highlights. Most visitors head straight for the Edvard Munch room, home to his most famous works, including *Madonna* and *The Scream*, which is located here rather than at the Munch museum itself. If this gallery was in London, Paris, or Rome there would be queues out of the door, but it's quite normal to find yourself all alone in the Munch room with one of the world's most famous artworks. Alone that is, apart from the security guard making sure you don't sneak a photograph.

The gallery is organized into a labyrinth of small rooms, each one representing a specific time period and/or style, so the rest of the highlights are dispersed throughout the building. Although the collection consists of predominantly Norwegian art from the Romantic era and more modern works, there is an impressive collection of works from French impressionists including Paul Cézanne, Édouard Manet, and perhaps the movement's most prolific practioner, Oscar-Claude Monet. Although each painting is

statue outside the National Gallery   Oslo Cathedral

captioned only with the title and artist, the theme of each room is described in detail in both Norwegian and English on a wall panel. This is well worth reading when first entering a room as it helps to set context.

Other must-sees include the self-portrait by Vincent van Gogh and the sumptuous French Salon, named for its original purpose of housing plaster copies of French sculptures. The French Salon's marbled stucco walls and fleurs-de-lis decals are now home to the gallery's cozy café. Opening times coincide with the gallery, although food is served only until 4pm.

NATIONAL MUSEUM OF ARCHITECTURE
(Nasjonalmuseet–Arkitektur)

The lesser known of the quartet of museums, yet my personal favorite, is the fabulous **National Museum of Architecture** (Bankplassen 3, 11am-5pm Tues.-Fri., noon-5pm Sat.-Sun.). The building itself is a great example of modern architecture, let alone the exhibits it guards inside. Architect Sverre Fehn refurbished the former Norwegian Central Bank building and achieved the delicate balance of restoring the Regency glory while adding in modern elements such as the glass pavilion to the rear. A film inside shows the story of the refurbishment. The museum is well suited for those who like the technical details of architecture, as plans and models of classical and modernist Norwegian buildings are everywhere.

MUSEUM OF CONTEMPORARY ART
(Museet for samtidskunst)

Immediately adjacent to the National Museum of Architecture, the **Museum of Contemporary Art** (Bankplassen 4, 11am-5pm Tues.-Fri., noon-5pm Sat.-Sun.) is home to thousands of artworks from 1945 to the present day. Photography and drawings are commonplace amid installations and digital media. A permanent exhibition from French-American

Louise Bourgeois (1911-2010) showcases her famous sculptural installations known as cells, most notably *Celle VIII*.

★ Oslo Opera House
(Operahuset)

With so much development going on at the waterfront **Bjørvika** neighborhood, you'll need to follow the signs to find the quickest route to the **Oslo Opera House** (Kirsten Flagstads plass 1, tel. 21 42 21 21, www.operaen. no). The striking angular design, somewhere between a glacier, ski slope, and a ship coming in to dock, connects the city to its people in spectacular fashion. The roof rises out of the water, allowing visitors the ability to walk right up to the top. From the top you can clearly see across the city, from the Holmenkollen Ski Jump to the Oslofjord islands, and you also get a front-row view of the striking new vertical development of offices and restaurants named Barcode.

The Italian marble, white granite, and glass structure shimmers beautifully in the summer sun, imposing yet inviting. With such a memorable design and views across the city and the fjord, you'd be forgiven for forgetting you're standing on top of an opera house. However, with free rooftop concerts held throughout the summer, you're unlikely to make that mistake.

Norwegian architect firm Snøhetta scooped many accolades for the design, including the 2008 culture award at the World Architecture Festival in Barcelona and the 2009 European Union Prize for Contemporary Architecture (Mies van der Rohe award). The interior is covered in oak to bring warmth in contrast to the coolness of the white exterior. A small café and shop are inside. A short distance into the fjord is the floating steel and glass art installation called *She Lies,* constantly moving with the waves and catching the light in a similar way to the giant windows of the Opera House itself.

Walking up to the roof of the Oslo Opera House is a must-do.

For further insights, a 50-minute guided tour (1pm Mon.-Fri., noon Sat., 100kr) gives you unique backstage access otherwise off-limits.

You don't get much for free in Oslo, so take advantage of one attraction with free entry close by. The **Norwegian Customs Museum (Norsk Tollmuseum)** (Tollbugata 1a, tel. 22 34 68 76, 11am-3pm Mon.-Fri., free) is appropriately housed in the old Customs headquarters. Original uniforms and items dating back more than 350 years are on display, alongside exhibits documenting the history of imports and exports to and from Norway. You won't need more than 20 minutes here.

Karl Johans gate and the Civic Center

Start your walking tour of Oslo's downtown from the biggest transit interchange in the city. Buses, trams, and people trundle across **Jernbanetorget** square all day while the T-Bane rumbles every few minutes through the tunnel beneath your feet. The statue of the tiger on the city square is one of the city's most photographed. At first glance one may wonder why Oslo is nicknamed the Tiger City (Tigerstaden), given the distinct lack of any orange-and-black striped animals roaming Scandinavia, yet statues of tigers appear all across the city.

The phenomenon actually comes from the 1870 poem *Last Song (Sidste sang),* in which the Swedish poet Bjørnstjerne Bjørnson described the dangerous city Oslo as a tiger fighting a horse representing the countryside. Hardly dangerous by world standings, but for a rural Norwegian the big city was seen as a ruthless place.

The Jernbanetorget square is useful to orient yourself by, with its tall tower marking the Ruter public transit information center, the start of **Karl Johans gate** (downtown's main artery), and just around the corner the sleek modern lines of the Opera House.

OSLO CATHEDRAL
(Oslo Domkirke)

First consecrated in 1697 and previously known as Our Saviour's Church, **Oslo Cathedral** (Karl Johans gate 11, 10am-4pm Mon.-Thurs., 4pm-6am Fri., 10am-4pm Sat.-Sun., free) is an active parish church for downtown Oslo and host of public events for the Royal Family and Government. After the Oslo and Utøya terror attacks of 2011, locals blanketed the streets outside with roses, notes, and candles right up to the tram tracks. Restored to its original baroque style, the interior includes the original pulpit, altar, and carved organ. Don't miss the adjacent Neo-Romanesque bazaar halls, built during the 19th century as butcher shops but today home to cafés and restaurants.

NORWEGIAN PARLIAMENT
(Stortinget)

Past the hustle and bustle of Karl Johans gate is the first of the impressive civic buildings built in the 19th century. The **Norwegian Parliament** (Karl

Johans gate 22, tel. 23 31 30 50, www.stortinget.no) is the Oslo Parliament building. The main entrance on Løvebakken was designed to face up to the Royal Palace. Unlike in many parliaments in the world, Norway's Plenary Chamber is located in the semicircular frontage with windows that open out onto the public square below.

Without getting elected to Parliament, the only way to get inside the building is on a tour. Free one-hour guided tours are held in English every Saturday morning at 11:30am on a first-come, first-served basis, with weekday tours added during July.

The tours look at the history of the building and politics in Norway and take you inside the Plenary Chamber, with plenty of good-natured humor about the Swedes and the Danes, of course. As the building is an active government building, it's advisable to check the website or tourist information to confirm the tours are running on your specific day of interest. Bookings are not possible except for groups, so wait in line outside the rear entrance on Akersgata; as long there are not 30 people (the maximum allowable) in front of you, you'll be fine. It's best to leave bags in your hotel, as you can expect airport-style security.

ROYAL PALACE
(Det kongelige slott)

Spend some time relaxing in front of the Parliament building in Eidsvolls plass, an urban park home to fountains and numerous events throughout the year, including a charming Christmas market in December. This section of Karl Johans gate is often used for processions and other public events, most notably on Norway's Constitution Day, May 17. The crowds fill the street as they approach the **Royal Palace** (Slottsplassen 1, tel. 22 04 87 00, www.kongehuset.no), the official residence of the Norwegian royal family. The palace is open to the public during the summer months but only on an official one-hour guided tour, on which you'll see various state rooms,

The Royal Palace stands at the end of Karl Johans gate.

the banqueting hall, and the palace chapel. They run four times daily in English from mid-June to mid-August starting at noon; book in advance.

A popular free attraction is the changing of the guard that takes place every day at 1:30pm in front of a camera-laden horseshoe of curious tourists. Erected 1845-1849, the Guardhouse is believed to be the oldest building in Norway built in the Swiss style.

A helpful link between downtown and the shopping district of Bogstadveien, the romantic **Palace Gardens (Slottsparken)** are worth a stroll at any time of year. The ponds, statues, and open spaces of the park look especially peaceful covered in snow.

IBSEN MUSEUM
(Ibsenmuseet)

Just behind the palace you'll find the **Ibsen Museum** (Henrik Ibsens gate 26, tel. 22 12 35 50, www.ibsenmuseet.no, 11am-6pm daily June-Aug., 11am-4pm daily Sept.-May, 100kr), dedicated to Norway's most famous playwright. At the turn of the 21st century, the interior of his former home was lovingly restored to the original colors and furniture, allowing visitors a glimpse into his mind as he wrote his dramatic final works. Exhibits from Ibsen's life can be viewed at any time, but the rooms of his home— the library, dining room, parlors, and study—are only available to view by joining a 30-minute guided tour. Available in English and Norwegian, the tours are held every hour on the hour up to one hour before closing. Book in advance to guarantee a spot, as groups are limited to 15.

To mark the importance of Ibsen's work to the Norwegian language, the sidewalks from the Grand Hotel to the museum feature 69 steel quotations inscribed into the ground from some of his most loved characters.

Waterfront

Until the construction work around the Oslo Opera House is complete, **Pipervika** remains Oslo's primary waterfront area, with a mix of old and new architecture.

AKERSHUS FORTRESS
(Akershus Festning)

Akershus Fortress might look familiar—it was the inspiration for the castle in the Disney film *Frozen*. A monument to Oslo's history, the fortress has played an important role in the city's fortunes since its construction in medieval times. Turned into a state-of-the-art palace in the 17th century by King Christian IV, the fortress successfully defended all sieges before becoming a prison in the 18th century.

During World War II, the German Wehrmacht occupied the fortress. The Norwegian prisoners were moved and the Germans used the fortress as a prison of their own for those opposed to the Nazi system. Needless to say, conditions were poor, the fortress earning the nickname "Death's waiting room" from locals. After inmates attempted to escape, conditions deteriorated even further, as all furniture and bedding were removed.

The fortress is still an active military area, but the grounds are open to the public until 9pm daily. A small **visitor center** (tel. 23 09 39 17, 11am-4pm Mon.-Fri., noon-5pm Sat.-Sun., free) tells the story of the fortress from medieval castle to war prison. The grounds offer visitors a terrific vantage point of the modern Aker Brygge development and the Oslofjord.

NORWEGIAN ARMED FORCES MUSEUM
(Forsvarsmuseet)

The **Norwegian Armed Forces Museum** (tel. 23 09 35 82, www.forsvarets-museer.no, 10am-5pm daily May-Aug., 10am-4pm Tues.-Sun. Sept.-Apr., free) traces Norwegian military history from the days of the Vikings right through to the present day. The unions with Denmark and Sweden are explored, along with the sea battles of World War II.

RESISTANCE MUSEUM
(Norges Hjemmefrontmuseum)

Located next to a memorial to Norwegians executed during World War II, the **Resistance Museum** (tel. 23 09 31 38, 10am-4pm Mon.-Fri., 11am-4pm Sat.-Sun., longer hours June-Aug., 60kr) chronicles the domestic fight against the Nazi occupation. Most of the original documents, newspapers, posters, and audio recordings that document the struggle are of course in Norwegian, and while written explanations in English are available, it's only worth the entrance fee if you're a real war history buff.

CHRISTIANIA TORV

A few minutes north of Karl Johans gate is the grid-style layout of the **Kvadraturen** district. Make time to pass through the heart of Kvadraturen, the cobbled square of **Christiania Torv.** Surrounded by a picturesque

Akershus Fortress

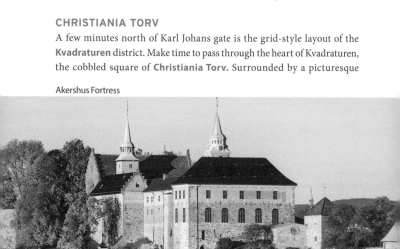

Nobel Peace Prize

Unlike all the other Nobel Prizes, which are awarded in Stockholm, the Nobel Peace Prize is awarded every November in Oslo. The prestigious annual award is intended to recognize those who have "done the most or the best work for fraternity between nations, for the abolition or reduction of standing armies, and for the holding and promotion of peace congresses."

Notable Winners

The first winners in 1901 were Switzerland's Henry Dunant, for his role in founding the Red Cross, and France's Frederic Passy, for being one of the main founders of the Inter-Parliamentary Union and also the main organizer of the first Universal Peace Congress.

Other notable winners include Nelson Mandela, Mother Teresa, Aung San Suu Kyi, Theodore Roosevelt, and Desmond Tutu. Organizations are also eligible for the award. Doctors Without Borders took the prize in 1999. In 2012 the European Union took the honor for "over six decades contributed to the advancement of peace and reconciliation, democracy, and human rights in Europe."

Controversy

Despite the award's prestige, it has not been without its controversy. In 1973 Henry Kissinger and Lê Đức Thọ were awarded the Nobel for their efforts in negotiating the Paris Peace Accords, although fighting continued on to 1975.

Lê Đức Thọ refused to accept the award, and two members of the Norwegian Nobel Committee members resigned in protest. Other controversial winners include Yasser Arafat and Barack Obama, the latter saying he did not feel deserving of the award, which was announced just nine months after he took office.

The prize has also caused controversy for its omissions. "The greatest omission in our 106-year history is undoubtedly Mahatma Gandhi," said Geir Lundestad, secretary of the Norwegian Nobel Committee in 2006. "Gandhi could do without the Nobel Peace Prize. Whether the Nobel committee can do without Gandhi is the question."

collection of original buildings from the 17th century, amid the cobbled roadway and centuries-old buildings, you'll find a fountain sculpture of a hand pointing downward. This marks the spot where King Christian IV chose to rebuild Oslo after a fire destroyed the old town in 1624. You won't be the first visitor to repeat his alleged words, "The new town will lie here!" while pointing to the ground!

MINI BOTTLE GALLERY

Hidden away in the Kvadraturen district is the **Mini Bottle Gallery** (Kirkegata 10, tel. 23 35 79 60, noon-4pm Sat.-Sun., www.minibottlegallery.com, 85kr), one of the city's most curious museums. Over 12,500 miniature bottles are on display in various installations, with a further 40,000 kept in a secure vault. Needless to say, it's the world's largest such collection. A popular venue for office parties and product launches, the Mini Bottle

Island Hopping in the Oslofjord

If the weather is kind to you, do as the locals do and head out to the small islands that dot the fjord in front of Oslo. Each island has its own distinctive character, from the beaches and history of Hovedøya to the residential vibe of Lindøya. Each island can be reached by small passenger ferries that run as part of the Ruter public transit system. They all leave from Rådhusbrygge 4, a small pier directly in front of Oslo City Hall. The ferry runs year-round, although departures are much less frequent outside the summer months, so check www.ruter.no for the latest timetable. Choose to stay on one island for the day, or design your own itinerary and hop between several.

Hovedøya

The largest and most popular of the islands, Hovedøya is great for swimming on its western beaches or playing games on the large open grassy area. The east of the island is dominated by a nature reserve and perfect for hiking. Historical monuments abound, including the ruins of a monastery founded by English Cistercian monks in the 12th century and burned down in 1532. You'll also find cannon batteries from the days when the island was used by the Norwegian army. A few steps from the jetty, the beautiful Lavetthuset is home to a gallery and small kiosk open during the summer.

Lindøya

Many of the Oslo residents that own one of the 300 summer cottages on Lindøya spend the whole month of July on the island. Peace and tranquility, yet just a 15-minute ferry ride from civilization. That population is served by a small shop and facilities including swimming areas and a football field.

Nakholmen

Similar to Lindøya, Nakholmen is a small island filled with 200 holiday cottages. Not the most interesting of the islands for travelers, but interesting to get an insight into the Norwegian summer house experience.

Gressholmen

The hilly island of Gressholmen is connected to Heggholmen and Rambergøya with causeways that form an important bay for sea birds. Home

Gallery is an intriguing concept, but a visit is only worth the entrance fee if you have a specific interest in bottles beyond their contents.

OSLO CITY HALL
(Rådhus)

Oslo City Hall (Fridtjof Nansens plass, tel. 23 46 12 00, 9am-4pm daily Sept.-June, 9am-6pm daily July-Aug., free) is easy to spot thanks to its distinctive twin brown towers. Despite its brutal post-war brick architecture, the City Hall is a popular building among locals, voted as Oslo's "structure of the 20th century."

The building is known for its bell tower, which rings out on the hour every hour. Featuring such classic composers as Edvard Grieg and Vivaldi, as well as more modern hits such as "Imagine" by John Lennon, the

to the picturesque Heggholmen lighthouse, the island is notable for holding Oslo's first main airport. Seaplanes landed here from 1927 to 1939, and the former airport is now a boatyard.

Bleikøya

One of the less frequented islands is also one of the more intriguing. Bleikøya is home to a former 19th-century sanatorium that housed children suffering with tuberculosis. A nature reserve occupies the northeastern part of the island, which is also home to a small World War II memorial.

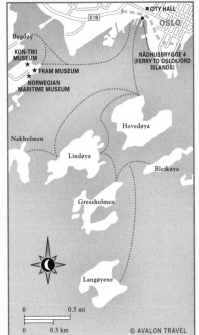

Langøyene

The only island that permits free overnight camping, Langøyene is a popular place to spend the long summer nights. The large beach, volleyball court, field for ball games, and small kiosk (summer only) attract a younger crowd, especially on weekends.

program has in recent years altered based on current events. In 2016, the bells rang out David Bowie's "Changes" to pay tribute to the iconic singer upon his death.

In addition to housing Oslo's city council and administrative offices, City Hall is home to an art gallery featuring predominantly Norwegian artists from the early 20th century. During June and July, free guided tours are held at 10am, noon, and 2pm. Tours are given in Norwegian or English depending on the makeup of the group. Given the number of tourists, it usually ends up being English. Tours in Spanish, German, and French are available upon request.

NOBEL PEACE CENTER
(Nobels Fredssenter)

The City Hall is known internationally for being the home of the Nobel Peace Prize ceremony every November. Next door is a museum chronicling the history of the award. At the heart of the Nobel Peace Center (Brynjulf Bulls plass 1, tel. 48 30 10 00, www.nobelpeacecenter.org, 10am-6pm daily, closed Mon. Sept.-May, 100kr) is the Nobel Field, a collection of digital screens surrounded by thousands of LED lights creating a unique ambience. Each screen contains the story of a Nobel laureate.

Other permanent exhibits tell the story of Alfred Nobel, while temporary exhibitions profile the most recent winners. Although by no means required, a guided tour from the ultra-knowledgeable guides is worth the extra planning. Tours in English are included in the ticket price and run at 2pm on weekends throughout the year, daily during the summer.

AKER BRYGGE

The old Aker shipyard dominated the area until its closure in 1982. Four years later, the first part of waterside development Aker Brygge opened its doors. Today, over 6,000 people work here and over 1,000 people call it their home. The offices, malls, and residences are linked by several public areas and a pier perfect for an afternoon stroll or people watching from the many restaurants, cafés, and ice-cream kiosks that line the route. A recent extension to Aker Brygge, Tjuvholmen (www.tjuvholmen.no) is a modern waterside development with a grim history. Thieves were executed here in the 18th century, and its name directly translates into English as the Thief's Island.

On the walk from Aker Brygge to Tjuvholmen you will pass the always-burning Eternal Peace Flame, dedicated to the city of Oslo by Sri Chinmoy in 2001 and designed to serve as a beacon of light and inspiration.

ASTRUP FEARNLEY MUSEUM OF MODERN ART
(Astrup Fearnley Museet)

Tjuvholmen is the sparkling new location of the Astrup Fearnley Museum of Modern Art (Strandpromenaden 2, tel. 22 93 60 60, www.afmuseet.no, noon-5pm Tues.-Wed. and Fri., noon-7pm Thurs., 11am-5pm Sat.-Sun., 120kr), a private collection of works that focuses on meaningful individual pieces rather than time periods or movements. In addition to the range of Norwegian contemporary artists, the collection has a strong American influence. The museum welcomes a regular carousel of touring exhibitions, including the likes of Alex Israel, Matthew Barney, and Cindy Sherman. Damien Hirst's diamond skull *For the Love of God* appeared here during the opening season.

Explore the waterside sculpture park right outside and you'll discover a small hidden beach. If you're in the mood for more artwork, take a few steps behind the Astrup Fearnley Museum to discover Galleri Haaken

Grünerløkka

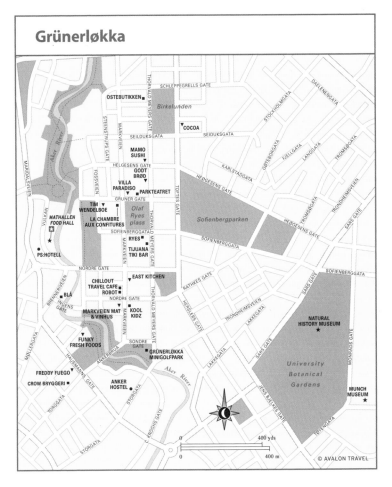

(Tjuvholmen allé 23, tel. 22 55 91 97, www.gallerihaaken.com, noon-5pm Wed.-Fri., noon-4pm Sat.-Sun., free), which showcases a range of Norwegian contemporary artists in a much more intimate setting. The curator is usually on hand to answer questions and will happily discuss all things art and all things Tjuvholmen.

GRÜNERLØKKA AND EASTERN OSLO

Most visitors to eastern Oslo go for shopping or nightlife rather than sight-seeing, but nevertheless there are some sights of note. A stroll northward along the Akerselva river bypasses Grünerløkka and takes you past for-mer mills and factories, many now converted to arts- and design-related trades. As you head farther, the feel of Oslo becomes more gritty, yet there are some sights to take in.

Munch Museum
(Munchmuseet)

Until its long-awaited move to a new high-profile location next to Oslo Opera House, the **Munch Museum** (Tøyengata 53, tel. 23 49 35 00, www. munchmuseet.no, 10am-4pm daily Oct.-June, 10am-5pm daily July-Sept., 100kr) remains open in Tøyen. Although the most famous works of Edvard Munch (1863-1944) are housed in the National Gallery, the museum still holds over 1,000 paintings, yet it is no ordinary art museum. During Munch's childhood, his mother died of tuberculosis and one of his younger sisters was diagnosed with mental illness. The museum reveals how this challenging childhood led to the dark psychological symbolism that defines much of his work. Munch once wrote, "My father was temperamentally nervous and obsessively religious to the point of psychoneurosis. From him I inherited the seeds of madness. The angels of fear, sorrow, and death stood by my side since the day I was born."

You'll never look at *The Scream* in the same way again.

University Botanical Garden
(Universitetets Botaniske hage)

The green lung of the otherwise urban eastern Oslo, the **University Botanical Garden** (Sars' gate/Monrads gate, tel. 22 85 17 00, 7am-9pm daily, free) offers a pleasant shortcut through to Grünerløkka. The fragrant garden, alpine garden, and old ornamental plants from Eastern Norway line your route. At the southwestern end, the Viking Garden displays the natural resources available during from the Viking Age. A caged hemp plant, herbs, rocks, and other plant life are all showcased within a Viking ship-themed outdoor exhibit.

North of the gardens is the **Natural History Museum (Naturhistorisk museum)** (Sars' gate 1, tel. 22 85 50 50, www.nhm.uio.no, 11am-4pm Tues.-Sun., 50kr), which encompasses a zoological museum popular with children. Known locally as Ida, the world's oldest complete primate skeleton has been on display since 2009, coinciding with the 200th anniversary of Darwin's birth and the 150th anniversary of the publication of *The Origin of Species*. The bone structure is so well preserved that historians can tell Ida is female and have placed the skeleton's age at an astonishing 47.8 million years. The lemur is likely to be the closest living relative alive today.

Ekeberg Sculpture Park
(Ekebergparken)

Farther out into Oslo's suburbs, **Ekeberg Sculpture Park** (Kongsveien 23, tel. 21 42 19 19, www.ekebergparken.no, free) doesn't have the crowds of Vigeland Park but offers just as much intrigue. The sculpture-laden natural forest and parkland offers outstanding views across the fjord and ever-expanding city. Salvador Dalí's *Venus de Milo aux Tiroirs* and Per Inge Bjørlo's *Inner Space VI—The Life Cycle* are two of the park's most visited spots, along with the very spot that inspired Edvard Munch to paint *The*

Vigeland Sculpture Park is one of Norway's most visited attractions.

the stave church from Gol at the Norwegian Museum of Cultural History

Scream. It is believed Munch's mentally ill sister Laura Catherine was a patient at the nearby asylum at the time. In 2013, Serbian filmmaker Marina Abramovic filmed 270 citizens of Oslo screaming out their emotions from Ekeberg Park in a disturbing, dramatic homage to Munch. A Scream-selfie here is hard to resist.

WESTERN OSLO
★ Vigeland Sculpture Park
(Vigelandsparken)

Wander the truly unique **Vigeland Sculpture Park** (Nobels gate 32, tel. 23 49 37 00, www.vigeland.museum.no, open daily, free) and get drawn in to the bizarre mind of Gustav Vigeland (1869-1943). More than 200 sculptures in bronze, granite, and wrought iron are on display in the park, which Vigeland himself designed. Walk from one end to the other in just 10 minutes, or spend an entire morning examining the human condition. Many sculptures take human form, and there is an eerie realism to them, not least the famous *Angry Boy,* its hand a different color due to the myth that if you touch it, you get good luck. (Park officials discourage this, though, because of deterioration to the sculpture.)

There are plenty of abstract sculptures too, such as the man being attacked by angry babies and the park's famous centerpiece, a 14-meter-high monolith consisting of 121 stone figures writhing around on top of one another in a desperate attempt to reach the sky. Critics of Vigeland say he was a Nazi sympathizer and his art is made up of fascist aesthetics, but it's hard to agree on a summer's day with the fountain flowing and locals mixing happily with tourists from every corner of the world.

The sculpture park is surrounded on all sides by the much larger **Frogner Park.** Oslo's biggest inner city playground is filled with locals walking dogs, barbecuing *pølser* (hot dogs), and playing Frisbee. It makes for a much nicer walk back to the transit interchange at Majorstuen once you're

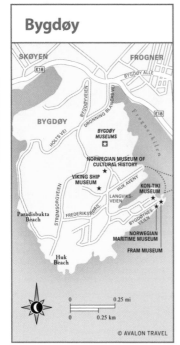

Bygdøy

done with Vigeland's work. Often skipped over by visitors, the **City Museum (Bymuseet)** (Frognerveien 67, tel. 23 28 41 70, www.oslomuseum.no, 11am-4pm Tues.-Sun., free) is set back in the park's southern corner and worth a look due to the fabulous 18th-century atmosphere of Frogner Manor. Inside the museum, the history of Oslo and the Frogner borough is examined largely through paintings and photographs, one of the biggest collections in Norway.

★ Bygdøy Museums

Whether by accident or design, Oslo's most distinctive museums of cultural history are bunched together on the otherwise wealthy residential peninsula of Bygdøy.

To reach Bygdøy, you can take bus 30, which runs a regular route from Jernbanetorget (outside Oslo Central Station) year-round, but the more interesting and quicker way is to take the ferry (Mar.-Oct.) from Pier 3 by City Hall. The first stop serves (by way of a short walk) the Norwegian Museum of Cultural History and the Viking Ship Museum, while the second stop drops you right outside the Kon-Tiki, Fram, and Norwegian Maritime Museums. Bus 30 stops outside all the Bygdøy museums.

The 10-minute ferry trip is quicker than the 20-minute bus trip, but a standalone ticket (35kr one-way, 55kr round-trip) is required from the booth before you board, as the regular public transit passes are not valid on the Bygdøy service. However, the ferry trip is complimentary for Oslo Pass holders.

NORWEGIAN MUSEUM OF CULTURAL HISTORY
(Norsk Folkemuseum)

If for some reason you're not heading out to the western fjords after your time in Oslo, then the **Norwegian Museum of Cultural History** (Museumsveien 10, tel. 22 12 37 00, www.norskfolkemuseum.no, 125kr) is a must-do for a taste of rural Norwegian life. The highlight of the center is a genuine medieval stave church from the town of Gol, which was relocated to Oslo by King Oscar II in the 19th century. Other farmsteads from all across the valleys of Norway have been acquired and relocated here, including a mustard yellow 19th-century farmhouse from Stiklestad with a refurbished interior to show how a busy farming family would have lived during the 1950s. Other notable highlights include the parsonage (1752) from Sogn and an open-hearth house, barn, and stable comprising the Setsedal farmstead (1739).

The park is open daily year-round, although the experience in the summer season from mid-May to mid-September is far richer. Open 10am-6pm, the open-air museum comes to life with hosts in traditional folk dress ready to show you their farmsteads and explain their lives to you, to the soundtrack of live folk music. Make it clear you're an English speaker and the hosts will happily switch languages.

Outside summer, the opening hours are drastically reduced to 11am-3pm (4pm on weekends), and the museum adopts a more serious demeanor, although there is still plenty to see for those with an interest in Norwegian culture.

VIKING SHIP MUSEUM
(Vikingskipshuset)

Neighboring the Museum of Cultural History, the **Viking Ship Museum** (Huk Aveny 35, tel. 22 13 52 80, 9am-6pm daily May-Sept., 10am-4pm daily Oct.-Apr., 100kr) is one of the most popular attractions on Bygdøy and with good reason. Three genuine Viking ship discoveries from Gokstad, Oseberg, and Tune are on display in the purpose-built building. Two of them are in spectacular condition, considering they were built in the 9th century. As much as the ships play a starring role, the exhibits around the periphery take you on an eye-opening journey into Viking life. Discover sledgehammers and household objects such as tools, textiles, and utensils that were used.

The ships provide the foundation for continuing research. The Gokstad grave was excavated in 1880 but until recently was never investigated using modern methods. A recent research project, Gokstad Revitalized, has revealed a marketplace at nearby Heimdalsjordet, providing yet more insight into the daily life of the Vikings.

KON-TIKI MUSEUM
(Kon-Tiki Museet)

In 1947, Norwegian explorer Thor Heyerdahl set sail from Peru on a hand-built raft called *Kon-Tiki*. He wanted to prove it was possible to sail to Polynesia as ancient myths told. After an 8,000-kilometer (5,000-mile) journey across the Pacific Ocean, his raft reached the Tuamotu Archipelago. His success backed up his theory that, contrary to popular belief that Polynesia was populated from west to east, there had been ancient contact from South America to Polynesia. Largely dismissed by modern anthropologists, Heyerdahl's theories and adventures nevertheless inspired an Academy Award-winning documentary movie. The **Kon-Tiki Museum** (Bygdøynesveien 36, tel. 23 08 67 67, www.kon-tiki.no, 10am-6pm daily

June-Aug., 10am-5pm daily Mar.-May and Sept.-Oct., 10am-4pm daily Nov.-Feb., 100kr) tells the tale of Heyerdahl and houses original vessels and equipment from his expeditions.

FRAM MUSEUM
(Frammuseet)

While you're in the mood for expeditions, explore a genuine polar vessel at the **Fram Museum** (Bygdøynesveien 36, tel. 23 28 29 50, www.frammuseum.no, 9am-6pm daily June-Aug., 10am-4pm daily Sept.-May, 100kr), adjacent to the Kon-Tiki Museum. The strongest wooden ship ever built, *Fram* survived journeys to both polar caps. Although principally focused on the vessel, the museum also profiles Norwegian polar explorers Fridtjof Nansen (who helped fund and specify the ship), Otto Sverdrup, and Roald Amundsen and the Scottish-Norwegian ship designer Colin Archer and has exhibits on polar bears and penguins.

NORWEGIAN MARITIME MUSEUM
(Norsk Maritimt Museum)

Next door to the Fram Museum is the **Norwegian Maritime Museum** (Bygdøynesveien 37, tel. 24 11 41 50, www.marmuseum.no, 10am-4pm Tues.-Sun., 100kr), which completes the series of museums of Bygdøy but is only worthwhile to those with a specific interest in maritime culture and history. Exhibits principally focus on the technical details of the shipping industry, although the hall of traditional boats and the maritime art gallery hold some interest.

NORTHERN OSLO

Northern Oslo is defined by its vast Nordmarka forest, where its hiking trails and lakes become the city's playground. But other than the ski arena, sightseeing opportunities are thin on the ground.

★ Holmenkollen Ski Arena
(Holmenkollen nasjonalanlegg)

The main attraction at **Holmenkollen Ski Arena** (Kongeveien 5, tel. 22 92 32 00, www.holmenkollen.com) is the **Holmenkollen Ski Jump (Holmenkollbakken),** visible from all across the city. This world-class sporting arena, which hosted the 1952 Winter Olympics and was rebuilt in 2011, is free to walk around, take in the remarkable views across the city, and feel your stomach churn at the thought of sailing off into the skies.

For the true Holmenkollen experience, take an elevator ride up the **ski jump tower** to see the views the jumpers get just before they set off. It's not for the faint-hearted. At the foot of the tower is the **Ski Museum (Skimuseet),** the world's oldest museum dedicated to skiing, profiles famous Norwegian polar explorers right through to present-day snowboarding. Never tried winter sports? **Simulators** allow you to give it a go in relative safety, although there's no guarantee you won't be embarrassed.

Northern Oslo

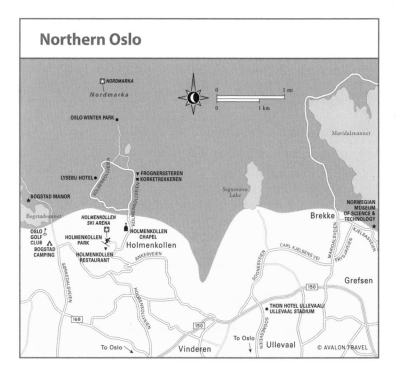

The ski jump tower, museum, and simulators are open 10am-4pm daily with extended hours of 9am-8pm from June to August. A 130kr ticket buys you entrance to the ski jump tower and museum, and the simulator costs 75kr, but the ski jump arena and gift shop are free to explore.

A word of warning: The only way to reach Holmenkollen by public transit is the T-Bane. As pleasurable as the Holmenkollen line is, a 10-minute uphill walk is required to reach the Ski Arena from Holmenkollen station. If you're visiting in the winter, check in advance at www.holmenkollen. com for any major events that will impede access for tourists. It's not uncommon to see Olympic-level athletes training in the biathlon arena and on the cross-country trails around Holmenkollen.

KOLLENSVEVET ZIP LINE

From April through October, Oslo's home of ski jumping plays host to another extreme activity. The **Kollensvevet Zip Line** (tel. 22 08 30 00, www. kollensvevet.no, 730kr) is an expensive yet exhilarating opportunity to get the same view as the professional ski jumpers who soar over the city. From mid-June through August, the line is open 11am-6pm Monday-Friday and noon-6pm Saturday-Sunday; outside those few weeks, hours are on weekends only. Arrive early to avoid a long wait, especially on weekends, when advance reservations are possible but only for an additional 500kr.

HOLMENKOLLEN CHAPEL
(Holmenkollen kapell)

Standing proudly overlooking the ski arena is **Holmenkollen Chapel** (Holmenkollveien 142, tel. 23 62 94 70), a traditional-looking church that hides a dark history. In 1993, musicians from Norwegian black metal band Emperor torched the original chapel, one of a series of church arsons in the early 1990s. The church was rebuilt a few years later to strongly resemble the traditional Norwegian stave churches, and is now one of the city's most popular venues for weddings. It's only open for services at 11am on Sunday.

Bogstad Manor
(Bogstad gård)

One of the few Norwegian country estates, **Bogstad Manor** (Sørkedalen 826, tel. 22 06 52 00, www.bogstad.no) is an oasis of calm just 10 kilometers (6 miles) northwest of Oslo. The history of the estate dates back to 1649, up until which the land had been cultivated and rented out to farmers. Morten Lauritzen bought the land from the Danish-Norwegian King Fredrik III and used the forested areas to boost the local timber trade.

Peder Anker, who became the first Norwegian prime minister in Stockholm in 1814 during the long union with Sweden, improved the estate during the 18th century. Inspired by the grand architecture of Versailles and Rome, he built a ballroom, collected paintings, and created Norway's first English landscape park, which housed exotic plants from all over the world inside greenhouses.

Guided tours (1pm Tues.-Sun. May-Sept.) of the museum are only available in Norwegian, but an English language booklet is provided. The fully restored 18th-century lakeside park is free to explore year-round. The café, gift shop, and small exhibition about the manor are open noon-4pm Tuesday-Sunday. To reach Bogstad Manor, travel to Røa T-Bane station and then take a 5-minute bus ride on route 41 or a 40-minute walk.

cross-country skiers at Holmenkollen Ski Arena

(Norsk Teknisk Museum)

If you are traveling with kids who love planes, trains, and automobiles, the **Norwegian Museum of Science & Technology** (Kjelsåsveien 143, tel. 22 79 60 00, www.tekniskmuseum.no, 11am-6pm daily mid-June to mid-Aug., 9am-4pm Tues.-Fri., 11am-6pm Sat.-Sun. mid-Aug. to mid-June, 150kr) is a must-visit attraction. The museum tells the story of Norway's development from an agrarian to an industrial society, and it's all done through bright, colorful, and interactive exhibits that are just plain fun. Founded over 100 years ago, the museum stays fresh by updating its exhibits on an annual basis. Because of its rather unusual location away from all other museums, it's best to combine a visit here with a hiking or swimming trip at nearby Sognsvann or a stroll along the Akerselva river.

VICINITY OF OSLO

A number of sights are all within easy reach of downtown Oslo by public transit.

Bærums Verk

In 1610, King Christian IV (of Denmark and Norway) founded an iron ore production facility 16 kilometers (10 miles) west of Oslo. Over 400 years later, **Bærums Verk** (tel. 67 13 00 18, www.baerumsverk.no, free) is now a thriving shopping destination. Verksgata is home to a blacksmith, glass-blower, textile shop, carpenter's workshop, and other traditional Norwegian crafts, while supermarkets and other shops service the neighboring village of the same name. The oven museum houses a unique collection of antique cast-iron ovens produced at the ironworks, from the baroque style of the 1700s up to the end of production in 1964.

The complex is open daily but opening hours vary for each shop. Go 10am-5pm (noon-4pm Sun.) to guarantee most places being open. From the end of November, the Christmas Street *(Julegaten)* opens every weekend, offering gift ideas, festive food, and entertainment, including leisurely reindeer-pulled sled rides.

To reach Bærums Verk, take bus 143, which has regular departures from Oslo Bus Terminal and stops right outside the complex. As the destination is outside the city of Oslo, a two-zone bus ticket is required for the 50-minute ride.

Eidsvoll House
(Eidsvollsbygningen)

Continue north past the airport on the E6 highway or the train and you come to **Eidsvoll,** a picturesque small village of wooden houses and churches. The real attraction here is the **Eidsvoll House** (Carsten Ankers veg 19, tel. 63 92 22 10, www.eidsvoll1814.no, 10am-5pm daily May-Aug., 10am-3pm Tues.-Fri., 11am-4pm Sat.-Sun. Sept.-Apr., 125kr), which marks the place where Norway became an independent country in 1814.

In April 1814, 112 elected representatives arrived at Eidsvoll and immediately divided in two. One group wanted complete independence for Norway, while the unionist half believed a union with Sweden was the best way forward. It took over a month for the battle to be settled and for a constitution to be drawn up and signed, declaring Norway an independent state.

Extensive restorations have turned the former manor house into a national monument to be proud of and where this history can be rightly remembered. In addition to the former manor itself, the visitor center highlights stories of global democracy from past and present, while the charming coffee house and gift shop are worthy stops.

Located 60 kilometers (37 miles) northeast of Oslo, Eidsvoll House can be reached by a 30-minute train journey from Oslo S station to Eidsvoll, followed by a 20-minute walk or a 5-minute bus ride on route 811. A three-zone ticket will be required. By car, the journey from downtown Oslo will take around 40 minutes.

Tusenfryd

While the name literally means *a thousand joys,* the Viking-themed **Tusenfryd** (Vinterbro, tel. 64 97 64 97, www.tusenfryd.no, from 299kr) theme park offers only 35 attractions—but kids will want to stick around for the day. Racing through the water rapids on Ragnarok and experiencing the 4D-motion ride Thor's Hammer are the must-dos, while two traditional roller coasters are worth the queues. The Formula-1 themed Speedmonster takes you from stationary to 90 kph (56 mph) in just two seconds, while speeds on the Thundercoaster top 100 kph (62 mph).

The park is open daily in June and July, plus most weekends in May and August. Opening hours vary and exceptions apply, so check carefully before you travel, especially as advance online booking secures the cheapest rate.

Located 20 kilometers (12.5 miles) south of Oslo, Tusenfryd can be reached in just 30 minutes on express bus 500, which leaves Oslo Bus Terminal half-hourly, or you can book park tickets through **Adventure Oslo** (tel. 41 14 64 74, adventureoslo.no) for inclusive bus travel from the city center.

Sports and Recreation

Oslo might be a cosmopolitan capital packed with art and culture, but that doesn't mean it's lacking in outdoor opportunities. Surrounded on all sides by forest and water, Oslo has plenty to offer those seeking an active outdoorsy break from the city.

TOURS

Walking Tours

If your time in Oslo is limited or you want to get your bearings on the first day of a longer stay, **Free Walking Tours** (www.freetouroslo.com) leave the tiger statue on Jernbanetorget square at 10am daily, with an additional 4pm tour Friday-Sunday. The 90-minute walk takes in the Oslo Opera House, Christiania Torv, Aker Brygge, Oslo City Hall, and all the attractions along Karl Johans gate.

While the tours are advertised as free, tips of around 50kr are expected by the English speaking-guide, who is usually an energetic university student. On weekends, groups can be uncomfortably large, but it's nevertheless a good way to orient yourself and decide what you want to take a closer look at during the afternoon.

Boat Tours

Båtservice Sightseeing (Rådhusbrygge 3, tel. 23 35 68 90, www.boat-sightseeing.com) runs a selection of fjord cruises from Pier 3 in front of the City Hall. The most popular is the two-hour **Fjord Sightseeing** (299kr) tour of the Opera House, Akershus Fortress, Aker Brygge wharf, and the inner Oslofjord islands. From mid-June to mid-August, there are six daily departures (starting at 10:30am), reduced to three in the shoulder season (Mar.-Sept.) and just two through the winter.

Their three-hour **Oslofjord Evening Cruise** (7pm most days June-Aug., 420kr) takes you out into the fjord in an old wooden sailboat with the sun low in the sky. Although the chance of taking to the water in a classic vessel is a tempting one, it's an expensive trip, given the only food served is a simple buffet of shrimp with bread and butter.

Inquire and buy tickets for both trips from the ticket booth on the pier or from Oslo Visitor Centre.

Bus Tours

When the weather is not so good, a bus tour from **HMK Sightseeing** (tel. 22 78 94 00, www.sightseeingoslo.com) is a good solution to see a lot of the city in relative comfort. If time is tight, the 2.5-hour **Panorama Tour** (270kr) ticks off the major attractions, including a brief stop for photos at Holmenkollen Ski Jump and a walking tour of the Vigeland Sculpture Park.

The longer **Full Day Sightseeing Tour** (420kr) also includes entrance to the Viking Ship Museum and your choice of the Fram Museum or Kon-Tiki Museum on the Bygdøy peninsula. Lunch is not included, so it's a wise move to bring your own; otherwise, you'll need to visit a museum cafeteria rather than the exhibits.

All tours are given in English, Norwegian, and German and start from behind City Hall.

HIKING

Oslo's city streets can be surprisingly quiet on a Saturday morning. That's because the locals head out to the hills. The forests to the north and east of the city are accessible by public transit, so within 30 minutes you can go from sipping a latte downtown to a 360-degree view of vast untouched forest.

★ Nordmarka

Just as much a symbol of the city as the Opera House or Royal Palace, the **Nordmarka** forest is the city's premier destination for hiking in the summer and fall and skiing in the winter and spring. The far-reaching trails climb hills, piercing a path through dense forest and around large lakes in a seemingly endless maze.

Reaching Oslo's wilderness is easy thanks to metro routes 1 and 6, which whisk you to Frognerseteren and Sognsvann stations, respectively, in under a half hour.

In contrast to the city streets, Nordmarka is bustling on Sunday. Norwegian families spanning multiple generations walk together and even come out of their shells a little. Try saying hello!

One of Nordmarka's most popular routes is the steady three-mile hike from **Frognerseteren** to the popular cabin at **Skjennungstua** (Ullevålseterveien 60, tel. 90 15 59 20, www.skjennungstua.no). The cabin's kiosk is staffed sporadically (most often 11am-4pm on Wednesdays and weekends), but there is also an unstaffed small cabin open year-round should you need to take shelter or grab a bite to eat. Payment for coffee and

The Nordmarka forest is a popular recreation spot year-round.

dried foods is made on an honesty policy, so carrying some cash on a hike is a wise idea. The hike to Skjennungstua is straightforward, albeit hilly, and should take around one hour.

You can reach the same destination from **Sognsvann,** but the distance is a little longer. For those after an easier stroll, a 45-minute loop around **Sognsvann lake** on the 3.7-kilometer (2.3-mile) cycle-free footpath is a great option, while heading east to the much larger **Maridalsvannet lake** is a great option for those on two wheels or who fancy a longer hike. The marked trail from Sognsvann to and around Maridalsvannet lake is 15.3 kilometers (9.5 miles) round-trip, with two mild ascents; the hike can take from three hours to an entire day, depending on your pace.

BIKING

Bicycles from **Oslo City Bike (Oslo Bysykkel)** (www.oslobysykkel.no) are available from over 100 stations across the city center and can be used for up to three hours at a time. Available from 6am to midnight from early April to late November, the bikes are only accessible by way of a season ticket costing 299kr per year.

A better alternative for tourists is the better quality rental bikes from **Viking Biking** (Nedre Slottsgate 4, tel. 41 26 64 96, www.vikingbikingoslo.com), available from 200kr per day. Bikes are available from April to October and the rest of the year weather-permitting. It's best to book online in advance. The company also offers guided sightseeing tours starting at 240kr. The daily Oslo Highlights tour is the most popular, but the River Bike tour opens up the Oslo missed by many and is highly recommended.

WINTER SPORTS
Skiing and Snowboarding

Less than a half-hour from downtown Oslo is the city's biggest winter sports facility, **Oslo Winter Park** (Tryvannsveien 64, tel. 22 14 36 10, www.oslovinterpark.no). Better known by locals by its former name Tryvann, the park can be reached by the free shuttle bus (or a short walk) from the Voksenkollen metro stop.

The season depends on snowfall, but in the majority of years, most of the 18 runs are open by December, thanks to artificial snow production facilities filling the gap. Once the season has started, snow production facilities and floodlights keep the park open 10am-10pm Monday-Friday and 10am-5pm Saturday-Sunday right through to mid-April.

A daily lift pass costs 400kr; access to the beginners' area is 200kr. Equipment rental runs at around 400kr, while lessons with patient English-speaking instructors are also available (695kr for 1hr, 1,570kr for 3hrs).

Snowboarders can use the park with a dedicated area, although for the international standard superpipe it's best to use the second entrance several miles away at Wyller. Take the metro to Røa and connect with the 41 bus. The long Wyllerløypa black run and express chair lift links the two sections of the park.

More serious skiers should consider the international standard slopes of the Hafjell and Kvitfjell resorts, just north of Lillehammer.

Tobogganing

Oslo's best toboggan run, **Korketrekkeren** (Frognerseteren, tel. 22 49 01 21, www.korken.no) sits on the hill that was formerly home to the 1952 Olympic bobsled and luge track. The 2,000-meter (6,562-foot) run starts at Frognesteren metro station and ends at Midstuen, where you can board the metro to start all over again. Daily sled rental from the outlet next to Frognerseteren restaurant costs 100kr, while the run itself is free to use. A day ticket for the metro is a wise investment.

SWIMMING

Swim for free in the Oslofjord or at selected lakes in Oslo's forests. The city's most popular beach is **Huk** on the Bygdøy peninsula, with the nearby **Paradisbukta** better suited for children. Both are within a short bus trip from downtown Oslo. On warm days, locals head for the islands of the inner Oslofjord, reachable by public ferry. **Hovedøya** is the best choice for sunbathing and swimming.

The most accessible lake open for swimming is at **Sognsvann** on the end of the metro line 6. Diving is possible and there is plenty of space for picnics in the surrounding forest and parkland.

For those who prefer more managed facilities, **Frognerbadet** (Middelthuns gate 28, tel. 23 27 54 50), an outdoor pool on the fringes of Frogner Park, is open from June to August, but you'll do well to find space on a hot summer weekend when queues to get in can snake down the street. The best alternative is the **Tøyenbadet** (Helgesens gate 90, tel. 23 46 22 90, 7am-7pm Mon.-Fri., 9am-7pm Sat.-Sun., 100kr) indoor public swimming center, which is open year-round. Tuesday and Thursday mornings are reserved for local schools.

GOLF

The par-71 championship course at **Oslo Golf Club** (Ankerveien 127, tel. 22 51 05 60, www.oslogk.no) is set on the shores of Bogstad lake, with a small waterfall providing the backdrop to the 12th green. Norway's oldest golf club welcomes members of other clubs to use its facilities. A handicap certificate of at least 28 for men and 32 for women is required, and arrangements should be made in advance. Greens fees are 950kr, with a 15 percent discount available in the Norwegian holiday month of July.

For those who don't take their golf quite so seriously, **Grünerløkka Minigolfpark** (Søndre gate 1, tel. 22 38 00 27, www.minigolfparken.no, noon-8pm daily, 50kr) is a fun alternative for all. Set next to the Aker river, the 18 holes are open every day, weather permitting. Giant street chessboards can also be played (free).

SPECTATOR SPORTS

Soccer

The Oslo region boasts three clubs competing in the Norwegian Premier League, with games taking place March through October. The **Vålerenga Fotball** (www.vif-fotball.no) team currently plays at the national **Ullevaal Stadion** (Sognsveien 75), three kilometers (two miles) north of downtown Oslo, although they are scheduled to move to their own purpose-built 18,000-capacity stadium at their traditional home in the east of the city in time for the 2018 summer season.

Their biggest local rivals are **Lillestrøm SK** (www.lsk.no). Their **Åråsen Stadion** holds 12,250, and with an average attendance of half that, tickets are available for almost all games on the day. It's 16 kilometers (10 miles) northeast of Oslo and an easy train ride from the capital.

Since returning to the top tier of Norwegian football in 2013, family-friendly **Stabæk** (www.stabak.no) enjoyed something of a renaissance under Bob Bradley, former boss of the U.S. men's national team. Their small **Nadderud Stadion** (Haukeveien) is not the grandest sporting arena but is within walking distance of Bekkestua metro station, 10.5 kilometers (6.5 miles) west of downtown Oslo.

Ice Hockey

Ice hockey in Norway is a popular winter sport, yet the domestic teams lack international success when compared to their Nordic neighbors. Still, while the crowds are orders of magnitude less than what you can expect at an NHL game, the **Vålerenga Hockey** (www.vif-hockey.no) team attracts anything from a few hundred to a few thousand spectators, who get a great view of the action at the asymmetrical and somewhat dated **Jordal Amfi** (Jordalgata 12) arena, originally built for the 1952 Winter Olympics. The arena is in the picturesque Kampen neighborhood just 2.5 kilometers (1.5 miles) east of downtown Oslo, and easy to reach on foot, by T-Bane, or by bus.

American Football

As evidenced by more and more NFL games taking place in London, American football is growing in popularity across the Atlantic. The trend is mirrored in Norway, where a thriving amateur league is capturing the interest of both American expats and Norwegians. The **Oslo Vikings** (www.oslovikings.com) play their home matches in front of decent crowds at Frogner Stadion in Majorstuen, while the **Vålerenga Trolls** (www.viftrolls.no) play next to the ice hockey stadium at Jordal.

Entertainment and Events

NIGHTLIFE

Due to Norway's high taxes on alcohol, the nightlife scene in Oslo is not as thriving as in many European cities. Norwegian youths will typically host a gathering at home called a *vorspiel* (fun fact—this comes from the German word for foreplay) before heading out to a bar or club for the final few hours.

As almost all clubs and bars must stop serving alcohol at 2am, there will be no dancing the night away in Oslo. Most locals prefer to get up early in the morning and head to the hills for skiing or hiking. This means that nightlife can seem subdued, but if you're looking for an after-dinner drink, you nevertheless have options.

Oslo is known for its brown bars—English-style pubs that focus on beer, often showing sport—while the gastropub phenomenon has spread across Oslo like wildfire.

The city's liveliest nightspots tend to center around Youngstorget and Grünerløkka. Covers are not common except for live concert venues and dedicated nightclubs, where you can expect to pay at least 100kr. Dress code is surprisingly casual in most venues except for the most exclusive spots. Age limits tend to be high, and it's not uncommon to see those under 23 turned away from clubs unless they happen to know the door staff.

Downtown

Techno-heads need look no further than intimate dance venue **The Villa** (Møllergata 23-25, tel. 93 25 57 45, www.thevilla.no, 11pm-3am most Friday and Saturday nights), one of Oslo's top underground nightspots. Appearances from the likes of Guy Gerber, Debbie Harry, and Bonobo frequently see hour-long queues along Møllergata. Farther up the street, the basement nightclub at **Revolver** (Møllergata 32, tel. 22 20 22 32, www.revolveroslo.no, 10pm-3am Fri.-Sat.) hosts regular local bands that lean toward the heavier side of rock.

The bared-down interior of **Himkok** (Storgata 27, tel. 22 42 22 02, 5pm-3am Sun.-Thurs., 3pm-3am Fri.-Sat.) is home to a microdistillery proving immensely popular with those in the know. In-house spirits, cocktails, and craft ciders from around the world are the reward for those who wait in the weekend queues. The same owners run the nearby **Crow Bryggeri** (Torggata 32, tel. 21 38 67 57, www.crowbryggeri.com, 3pm-3am daily), a microbrewery with a vast selection of imports also on offer. Its industrial decor attracts a curious mix of hipsters alongside those who are there for the beer. A similar crowd frequents the exposed metalwork, bare-brick walls, and giant wall maps at Grønland's **Oslo Mekaniske Verksted** (Tøyenbekken 34, tel. 45 23 75 34, www.oslomekaniskeverksted.no, 3pm-2am Mon.-Fri., 1pm-2am Sat.-Sun.), a bar where beers and wines are the staple choices. Because the venue allows patrons to bring their own food, the nearby pizza places do a roaring trade.

Prices are lower at the down-to-earth **Cafe Sør** (Torggata 11, tel. 41 46 30 47, www.cafesor.no, 10am-midnight Mon.-Thurs., 10am-3am Fri.-Sat., 11am-midnight Sun.), which attracts an eclectic mix of old and young, locals and visitors to its downtown location. Get there early to snag a spot on the street-facing terrace.

The word quirky was invented for **Cafe Laundromat** (Underhaugsveien 2, tel. 21 38 36 29, www.laundromat.no), a bar, café, and library tagged on to a laundromat in the Bislett neighborhood northwest of downtown (take the tram or bus to Bislett Stadion). Freshen up your traveling clothes while reading from the vast library and sampling one of the various whiskeys, tap beers, or cocktails. You may just need that extra rinse cycle.

Grünerløkka and Eastern Oslo

Start your evening out in Grünerløkka with a beer in the rockabilly-themed bar **Ryes** (Thorvald Meyers gate 59, noon-1am Sun.-Tues., noon-3am Wed.-Sat.), before heading across the square to the former cinema turned bar and concert venue **Parkteatret** (Olaf Ryes plass 11, tel. 22 35 63 00, www.parkteatret.no, 11am-late daily). The bar is a lively place for music lovers, regardless of whether you have tickets to whoever is playing in the adjacent concert venue. If live music isn't your thing, perhaps you'll prefer the Mexican atmosphere and rum- and tequila-packed cocktails of the **Tijuana Tiki Bar** (Thorvald Meyers gate 61, tel. 90 07 71 91, www.tijuana.no, noon-4am Mon.-Sat., noon-midnight Sun.).

There's usually a band on most nights at intimate riverside club **Blå** (Brenneriveien 9, www.blaaoslo.no, hours vary). Almost part of the furniture, the funky 18-person Frank Znort Quartet play a free jazz/blues show every Sunday afternoon prior to their main evening gig. These Sunday sessions are an Oslo institution and the laid-back atmosphere draws many people back week after week. Legendary cocktail bar **Pigalle** (Grønlandsleiret 15, tel. 24 10 19 99, 4pm-1am Tues.-Thurs., 4pm-3am Fri.-Sat.) has enjoyed a long-overdue makeover and now sports a modern interpretation of a 1920s art-deco establishment, complete with plants, custom-designed furniture, and an overhauled drinks menu.

Western Oslo

Head to Frogner if you like your nightlife a little more high-brow, but be prepared to pay for the experience. Enjoy a glass or two of fizz at **Champagneria** (Frognerveien 2, tel. 21 08 09 09, 4pm-1am Mon.-Wed., 3pm-3am Thurs.-Fri., 1pm-3am Sat., 1pm-midnight Sun.). The rooftop terrace and focus on champagne, cava, and wine attract a more mature crowd. From here, take the short walk to the red carpet of swish nightclub **Nox** (Henrik Ibsens gate 100, tel. 22 55 40 00, www.clubnox.no, 11pm-3am Fri.-Sat.) to enjoy a glass of wine or classic cocktail in its lavish interior.

LGBT

Norway's cities are generally very accepting of LGBT lifestyle and thus there are only a few specific gay bars. You're likely to find as many LGBT couples in the bars of Grünerløkka as you are in the gay bars. Those bars are clustered together on a couple of streets downtown.

The first stop for many is Oslo's largest gay venue, **London Pub** (C. J. Hambros plass 5, tel. 22 70 87 00, www.londonpub.no, 3pm-3:30am daily), which offers a frankly bizarre mix of camp music, drag queens, and pool tables in an English pub-style basement bar. The upstairs nightclub (cover is charged) is underwhelming, so most patrons seeking a dance floor head over to the nearby **Elsker** (Kristian IVs gate 9, tel. 45 21 41 33, www.elsker-oslo.no, 6pm-3am Wed.-Sat.), an intimate bar with music so loud there's no point in even trying to strike up a conversation. Norway's only lesbian bar, **So** (Arbeidergata 2, www.so-oslo.no, 7pm-1am Thurs. and Sun., 9pm-3am Fri.-Sat.), is a popular alternative combining a dance floor with a quieter lounge area. Both Elsker and So run regular quiz nights and other events that may make them a dance floor-free zone for an evening.

A chilled-out brasserie by day, **Ett Glass** (Rosenkrantz' gate 13, tel. 91 77 53 90, www.ettglass.no, 11am-1am Mon.-Tues., 11am-3am Wed.-Fri., noon-3am Sat., noon-1am Sun.) becomes a popular nightspot for cocktails once the kitchen closes at 10pm. Frequented by everyone gay, straight, and everything in between, the stylish bar is one of Oslo's most established.

The city's LGBT communities come together every June for **Oslo Pride** (www.oslopride.no), Norway's largest LGBT festival. Usually held in the public square in front of the City Hall, Oslo Pride's highlight is the parade that makes a very visible statement along Oslo's main drag, Karl Johans gate. The festival also has a serious side though, touching on literature, art, and political debates throughout its week-long program.

While not strictly an LGBT event, the Eurovision Song Contest is hugely popular within the LGBT community. Run by state broadcaster NRK, the annual **Melodi Grand Prix** (www.nrk.no/mgp) is held over several weeks in January to choose Norway's entry for the annual showcase of all things kitsch. The February final, usually held in Oslo, attracts as much interest as many major sporting events. Tickets are available to the public but sell out well in advance.

PERFORMING ARTS

Oslo in a music-loving city and there is live music somewhere in the city on any night of the week. The likes of Adele, Justin Bieber, and Rihanna play at the vast but soulless **Telenor Arena** (Widerheveien 1, www.telenorarena.no), while the smaller but much better-located **Spektrum** (Sonja Henies plass 2, www.oslospektrum.no) also welcomes major artists and events.

Smaller bands and shows are held almost every night at one of the three downtown venues part of the **Rockefeller** group (www.rockefeller.no), all located on Torggata. Tickets go fast for any international names, so be sure to check out any concerts you might want to attend in advance of your arrival.

The **National Theater (National Theatret)** (Johanne Dybwads plass 1, tel. 22 00 14 00, www.nationaltheatret.no) is an imposing 19th-century home to playwrights and artists built from private funds to mark the secession from Sweden. The writers of the opening performances, Ludvig Holberg, Henrik Ibsen, and Bjørnstjerne Bjørnson, are immortalized in statues out front, and their names are carved in the stonework on the front facade. Today the theater is Oslo's premier arts venue, hosting everything from Shakespeare to the International Ibsen Festival.

The **Oslo Philharmonic (Oslo Filharmonien)** (www.ofo.no), the city's symphony orchestra, has a proud history that can be traced back to the days of Edvard Grieg. Since 2013, Russian Vasily Petrenko has been chief conductor of the orchestra, which gives over 100 concerts a year, many at its home **Oslo Concert House (Oslo Konserthus)** (Munkedamsveien 14, tel. 23 11 31 11, www.oslokonserthus.no). In addition to the many performances from the city orchestra, the concert house hosts a Jazz Café on most Saturday afternoons in Glasshuset, for which tickets start at a very reasonable 125kr.

Home of the Norwegian National Opera and Ballet (Den Norske Opera & Ballett), **Oslo Opera House (Operahuset)** (Kirsten Flagstads plass 1, tel. 21 42 21 21, www.operaen.no) hosts regular free performances on its roof and in the café, alongside the scheduled program. The venue holds regular opera and ballet performances throughout the year.

Nordisk Film Kino runs seven cinemas across Oslo with international releases alongside Norwegian films. International films will often have Norwegian subtitles, and only children's films tend to be dubbed. If in doubt, ask in advance. The biggest of the cinemas is **Colosseum kino** (Fridtjof Nansens vei 8, Majorstuen), while **Klingenberg kino** (Olav Vs gate 4) is most convenient for those downtown.

FESTIVALS AND EVENTS

In recent years Oslo has become the festival capital of Scandinavia, with events coming thick and fast throughout the summer season. Yet the Norwegian capital isn't the place to find traditional Norwegian festivals. As an ambitious growing city, Oslo focuses on bringing the newest trends from around the world to its streets. Oslo rivals cities many times its size for the sheer number and diversity of its internationally focused festivals. From business and innovation to music and films from around the world, there's a festival in Oslo for it.

Constitution Day

There are parades in even the smallest village on May 17 to mark Constitution Day, celebrating the independence of Norway. Although not unique to Oslo, the capital's parade is certainly the biggest and best. Noted most of all for its absence of military, the parade is formed by children from every school across Oslo. They march along Karls Johans gate up to the Royal Palace, where the king and his family are waiting to greet them. Although a rare display of national pride from the Norwegians (you can't move two feet without encountering a Norwegian flag), foreigners are welcome observers and locals are only too pleased to share their day. Just be wary that almost all tourist attractions will be closed on May 17 and many restaurants are booked up weeks in advance.

Music Festivals

The SXSW of Scandinavia is how **By:larm** (www.bylarm.no) wants to be described, combining a music festival of largely unsigned or breaking acts from across Scandinavia with a conference on the latest industry trends. The conference element has grown massively in recent years and now covers many talks about digital trends and cultural talking points. Taking place across multiple venues over four days in early March, the music festival offers passes for the day or the entire event, which go on sale approximately three months beforehand.

The short summer season kicks off in early June with the one-day **Musikkfest Oslo** (www.musikkfest.no), where up to 30 outdoor stages quite literally fill the streets with music, all for free. A couple weeks later, **Norwegian Wood** (www.norwegianwood.no) takes place at Frogner Park with the likes of Bob Dylan, Sting, and Lou Reed having graced its stage. The festival tends to attract an older crowd for its three-day run.

August is the month for music lovers to visit Oslo, as festivals pack the calendar. Held at Tøyen Park, **Øya Festival** (www.oyafestivalen.no) has broadened its rock traditions in recent years with the likes of New Order, Kraftwerk, and Massive Attack joining the lineup, which also features many breakthrough Norwegian acts. Passes for the four-day mid-August event sell out months in advance, but availability of single-day tickets is better.

Also held in mid-August, **Oslo Jazz Festival** (www.oslojazz.no) is a

Øya Festival is the city's main contemporary music event.

week-long showcase of the best in Nordic jazz, with selected guests from overseas providing some bulk to the lineup. Finally, broaden your cultural horizons at **Mela** (www.mela.no), an annual performing arts festival featuring international rhythms with a strong Asian influence. The festival and its 300,000 attendees takes over Rådhusplassen in front of City Hall for one weekend in mid- to late August every year.

In mid-September, 17 of Oslo's arts institutions get together for the week-long **Ultima** (www.ultima.no), a contemporary music festival with a focus on high artistic quality that also features an international symposium.

Film Fra Sør

Screening over 100 films from Asia, Africa, and Latin America, **Film Fra Sør** (www.filmfrasor.no) brings quality films to the people of Oslo each fall. The organizers aim to reach the multicultural audience in Norway as well as expose Norwegians to new thoughts and debates about the southern hemisphere. To help achieve its artistic goals, the festival runs a fund to support film production in the non-western world. Held over 10 days in early October, screenings are individually ticketed, and tickets should be bought online in advance.

Shopping

DOWNTOWN

Downtown Oslo has malls aplenty, with **Oslo City** (Stenersgaten 1, tel. 81 54 40 33, www.oslocity.no, 10am-10pm Mon.-Fri., 10am-8pm Sat.) and **Byporten** (Jernbanetorget 6, tel. 23 36 21 60, www.byporten.no, 10am-9pm Mon.-Fri., 10am-8pm Sat.) directly opposite one another by Jernbanetorget square.

Fashion dominates the upscale mall that lies behind the restaurant strip at **Aker Brygge** (Bryggegata 9, tel. 22 83 26 80, www.akerbrygge.no, 10am-8pm Mon.-Fri., 10am-6pm Sat.).

You'll find Oslo's biggest bookstore, with a great selection of English language books, including many Moon titles, on the ground floor of the boutique-filled **Paleet** (Karl Johans gate 37-43, tel. 23 08 08 11, www.paleet.no, 10am-8pm Mon.-Fri., 10am-6pm Sat.), between Parliament and the Royal Palace.

GRÜNERLØKKA AND EASTERN OSLO

The vibrant district of Grünerløkka is the number one destination for vintage clothing and trinkets. You'll find boutiques, thrift stores, and everything in between on the grid system of streets. During the summer, Birkelunden square hosts a Sunday thrift market (noon-6pm), while the buildings around the Blå nightclub host a Sunday crafts market (noon-5pm) year-round.

Head to the **Chillout Travel Cafe** (Markveien 55, tel. 22 35 42 00, www.chillout.no, 10am-7pm Mon.-Fri., 10am-6pm Sat., noon-6pm Sun.) for a better range of outdoor clothing and hiking/camping equipment than you'll find in most sports stores, plus traveling advice from the seasoned traveler staff. Before you move on, mull over the extensive travel library in the basement lounge with a chili mocha from the in-store café.

Next door, behind the funky exterior of **Robot** (Korsgata 22, tel. 22 71 99 00, 11am-6pm Mon.-Fri., 11am-5pm Sat., noon-5pm Sun.) you'll find a small selection of vintage clothes and retro bags, with staff that know exactly what will suit you. As the name suggests, **Kool Kidz** (Markveien 56, tel. 90 19 28 25, www.koolkidz.no, noon-6pm Mon.-Fri., 11am-5pm Sat., 1pm-5pm Sun.) is a boutique that specializes in children's clothes. Slogan-filled tees and designer dresses sit alongside pop-up books and other gifts, with many exclusive Scandinavian brands stocked.

The neighborhood is also great for food shopping. In addition to the goodies available at the Mathallen food hall, the French-inspired **La Chambre aux Confitures** (Olaf Ryes plass 6, tel. 92 16 19 17, 11am-6pm Mon.-Sat.) is stacked floor-to-ceiling with specialty jams and preserves, while **Ostebutikken** (Thorvald Meyers gate 27, tel. 22 37 80 65, 4pm-10pm Mon.-Tues., noon-10pm Wed.-Sun.) has a busy cheese counter frequented by locals and is a great choice for helping to compose a picnic to enjoy in one of the nearby parks.

WESTERN OSLO

Trailing off from behind the Royal Palace up toward Majorstuen is Oslo's most exclusive shopping street. Most stores on **Hegdehaugsveien** and **Bogstadveien** (essentially two different stretches of the same street) are open 10am-6pm Monday-Saturday, but almost all are closed on Sunday.

Sport meets fashion at **Tatler** (Bogstadveien 2, tel. 22 60 29 58, www.tatler.no), where shelves are filled with Ralph Lauren, Acne, Canada Goose,

Chillout Travel Cafe has an excellent travel bookshop.

Ugg, and Gudrun. Be wearing one of these brands when you enter or you'll get a few dirty looks. A few steps away is the flagship store of Scandinavian menswear retailer **Volt Magasin** (Hegdehaugsveien 30b, tel. 23 21 85 97), and there are many luxury brand stores, such as **Lacoste** (Hegdehaugsveien 34, tel. 22 56 69 00). A **farmers market** (noon-6pm) takes place on leafy Valkyrie plass most Saturdays.

Food

DOWNTOWN
Cafés and Light Bites

The flagship outlet of **United Bakeries** (Karl Johans gate 37-43, tel. 94 02 41 02, 7:30am-8pm Mon.-Fri., 9am-6pm Sat., 11am-5pm Sun.) is the best downtown choice for an on-the-go breakfast or a quick bite at any time of day. Fresh pastries are always on offer, and although the tables around the service area might seem cramped, there's plenty more seating out back.

Perfectly positioned for a stop before or after a visit to Akershus Fortress, **People & Coffee** (Rådhusgata 21, tel. 40 29 62 22, www.peopleandcoffee.no, 7am-6pm Mon.-Fri., 11am-6pm Sat.-Sun.) is an independently run coffee shop with an international vibe thanks to its mix of regulars from the business district and passing tourists. Sandwiches, salads, and soups are served all day, although most people just grab a quick coffee to go.

Traditional Scandinavian

With new Nordic flavors all the rage, traditional Norwegian cooking is surprisingly hard to find on the streets of Oslo. Get your fill of salted meats and boiled potatoes in the unique atmosphere of **Dovrehallen** (Storgata 22, tel. 22 17 21 01, 10am-midnight Mon.-Thurs., 10am-3am Fri.-Sat., noon-midnight Sun., 135-199kr), a traditional Norwegian dining hall hidden up some stairs from a busy rundown shopping street. On Friday and Saturday evenings, a live folk band entices the clientele—mainly elderly Norwegian couples—onto the dance floor.

New Nordic

See for yourself why Esben Holmboe Bang is the new star of new Nordic at ★ **Maaemo** (Schweigaards gate 15b, tel. 22 17 99 69, www.maaemo. no, 6pm-midnight Tues.-Fri., noon-midnight Sat.), which leads the way in Oslo's fine dining revolution, scooping up Michelin stars like they're going out of fashion. The simple, clean interior is deliberately designed to put the focus on the food, which brings the best Scandinavian seasonal ingredients from biodynamic farms together on a bewildering series of plates. Call several months in advance to stand a chance of booking a table, and expect to cough up around 4,000kr per person (including wine).

Arctic cod dominates the menu at **Gamle Rådhus** (Nedre Slottsgate 1, tel. 22 42 01 07, www.gamle-raadhus.no, noon-4pm and 5pm-10pm Mon.-Fri., 5pm-10pm Sat., 289-435kr), where they try perhaps a little too hard to blend French classic with new Nordic. The restaurant is set inside Oslo's original 17th-century city hall. Snag a table out in the secluded garden from May through August.

Seafood

Down at Aker Brygge, the rustic **Rorbua** (Stranden 71, tel. 22 83 64 84, www.rorbua.as, noon-10pm Tues.-Sat., noon-9pm Sun.-Mon., 179-329kr) is perhaps the only unpretentious spot on the whole promenade, save for the golden arches of course. Taking its design cues from a northern Norwegian fisherman's cottage, the lively pub has a menu to match, with fish soup the best budget option. For an introduction to the flavors of the ocean, the northern Norwegian plate includes marinated trout, stockfish, elk sausage, and smoked whale.

Named after the region from where much of its produce originates, **Lofoten** (Stranden 75, tel. 22 83 08 08, www.lofoten-fiskerestaurant.no, 11am-11pm Mon.-Sat., noon-10pm Sun., 200-425kr) serves a similar selection to Rorbua but in a modern setting where white tablecloths and wine glasses trump long wooden tables and beer glasses.

American

Thanks to its location between the train and bus stations, the rowdy rock-themed **Fiasco** (Schwegaardsgate 4, tel. 47 17 40 00, www.fiasco.no, 11am-midnight Mon.-Thurs., 10am-2am Fri., 11pm-2am Sat., noon-midnight Sun., 130kr) is a popular after-work spot with locals. A decent range of draft and bottled beers is on offer at reasonable (for Oslo) prices. The burgers are delicious but, as the kitchen is tagged on to the bar almost as an after-thought, be prepared for a wait. While the burgers are decent value, it's a bit mean spirited to charge an extra 35kr for sides. For something a little different, try the bacon jam burger.

The light, airy interior of ★ **Pinerolo Americano** (Henrik Ibsens gate 60, tel. 22 55 00 47, www.pinerolosolli.no, 4pm-10pm Mon.-Sat., 199kr) brings a touch of New England elegance to the heart of Oslo, just a stone's throw from the old U.S. Embassy. Compose your own two-course Boston (445kr) or three-course New York (545kr) menu, on which the seafood-based starters are especially appetizing. Order some mac-and-cheese, truffle fries, and chili corn on the cob to share; an after-dinner Hamptons Sour will complete your dose of Americana in this good-value eatery.

The 200-gram (nearly half-pound) handmade patties at gourmet fast-food outlet **Burger Joint** (Holmens gate 3, tel. 21 08 22 75, www.burger-joint.no, 11am-10pm Mon.-Thurs., 11am-midnight Fri., noon-midnight Sat., noon-10pm Sun., 175kr) are up there with the best in Norway, but it's a bit mean-spirited to charge separately for fries. Double up on your burger for an extra 75kr. The limited seating in this intimate venue means eating in can be a challenge, but there are plenty of places to sit on the nearby Aker

Brygge wharf. Alternatively, grab a table at the neighboring Beer Palace, from where you can order and eat from the Burger Joint menu.

Asian

The Thai café **Rice Bowl** (Youngs gate 4, tel. 22 41 20 06, www.ricebowl.no, noon-10pm Mon.-Sat., 2pm-9pm Sun., 150kr) is filled with locals all day due to the rare combination of great prices and decent portion sizes. The informal café atmosphere encourages swift eating despite plenty of seating. No alcohol is served, so if you prefer a beer with your food, head to the nearby family-run Vietnamese **Far East** (Bernt Ankers gate 4, tel. 22 20 56 28, 1pm-midnight daily, 175kr), although be wary of the sometimes slow service and, unusually for Oslo, a lack of spoken English by the (often just one) wait staff. The restaurant bears clear signs of not being an original restaurant and has a somewhat jumbled approach to decor.

Upscale Vietnamese and Thai restaurant **Mr Bay** (Olav Selvaags plass 1, tel. 22 83 22 01, 11am-midnight Mon.-Fri., 1pm-midnight Sat., 1pm-9pm Sun., 279kr) is a fashionable alternative on Tjuvholmen. Hungry diners can tackle the vast 10-course chef's menu (789kr pp), which is served tapas style all at once. From the regular menu, the succulent tenderloin is an especially good platform for the kitchen's authentic eastern spices. The restaurant boasts an impressive wine list, and advance booking is essential.

Caribbean

Lemon, lime, and ginger are used to great effect in this popular Caribbeanesque restaurant that's more themed than authentic. The colorful **Lemongrass** (Kristian Augusts gate 14, tel. 22 20 12 22, www.lemongrass.no, 4pm-10pm Sun.-Thurs., 4pm-11pm Fri.-Sat., 259kr) specializes in chicken (jerk or nut) and lighter fish dishes, such as sea bass, which work well with the citrus accompaniments. The flavor-packed mango and avocado salad is a popular choice for vegetarians. The restaurant is often open 11am-3pm offering a slimmer lunch menu, while after 10pm it transforms into an upscale nightspot.

Indian

Attentive service and authentic Indian food rarely go hand-in-hand in Norway, so ★ **IndiSpice Restaurant** (Welhavens gate 2, tel. 22 20 96 08, www.indispice.no, 4pm-10pm daily, 239kr), just a few streets away from the Royal Palace, is a real find. Servings are generous, so skip starters and go straight for the mains. Ginger slivers and punchy coriander add a freshness to the plates, which the staff will go to great lengths to ensure are served at a heat level you are comfortable with. The upscale interior, mood lighting, and stylish furniture add a touch of class rarely seen in Norway's Indian restaurants. Reservations are recommended for weekends.

The outstanding Persian-inspired ambience of **Mister India** (Dronningens gate 19, tel. 22 41 42 00, www.mister-india.no, 3pm-10pm Mon.-Sat., 3pm-9pm Sun., 249kr), just steps from Karl Johans gate at the heart of downtown Oslo, is a worthy alternative. The menu of lesser-known dishes, such as the lamb-based *achari gosht* curry and vegetarian-friendly *kaikari kuruma,* makes a welcome change from the norm.

Mexican

The Norwegian take on Tex-Mex is popular throughout the capital, but you have to look a little harder for something a little more authentic. The small *lucha libre* (Mexican wrestling) themed **Freddy Fuego** (Hausmanns gate 31a, tel. 40 06 64 28, www.freddyfuego.no, 11am-9pm Tues.-Sun., 120kr) is a burrito bar with fresh salsas made daily. The lines can be out the door during the early Norwegian lunchtime, but head there after 1pm and you should walk straight up.

Tacos and quesadillas fill the menu at **Taqueria** (Karl Johans gate 39, tel. 23 89 86 40, www.taqueria.no, 11am-11pm Mon.-Thurs., 11am-midnight Fri.-Sat., 120kr), and although the servings are on the small side, the prices are reasonable considering its prime location on Karl Johans gate. Despite the efforts of the decor, the atmosphere bears little resemblance to a bustling Mexican taco stand and feels all too Norwegian, so you may prefer to get takeout.

Vegetarian

Tucked away behind City Hall, the **Fragrance of the Heart** (Fridtjof Nansens plass 2, tel. 22 33 23 10, 7:30am-6pm Mon.-Wed., 7:30am-7pm Thurs.-Fri., 10am-7pm Sat., 11am-5pm Sun.) café serves vegetarian and vegan soups, pies, sandwiches, and wraps. They actively promote the Lemon Diet, a supposedly effective cleansing diet based around a cocktail of water, lemon juice, syrup, and cayenne pepper—but you won't be turned away if you all want is a caffeine hit, as this is an airy coffee shop first, vegetarian café second.

Although billed as a restaurant, the atmosphere at the Norwegian Centre for Design and Architecture's **Funky Fresh Foods** (Hausmannsgate 16, tel. 45 91 57 79, 10am-5pm Mon.-Tues., 10am-10pm Wed.-Fri., noon-10pm Sat., noon-7pm Sun., 99-179kr) is that of a fast food café. The limited menu features freshly made hamburgers and salads alongside milkshakes. The riverside location makes this a great vegan lunch option for those heading to or from Grünerløkka.

A quick pit stop for those downtown, **Proletaren** (Torggata 7, tel. 91 65 18 65, 11am-6pm Mon.-Sat., closed in July, 50kr) offers a largely vegetarian menu of take-away soups. The six soups rotate regularly, but expect the likes of spinach and squash, carrot and lentil, mung bean, and cream of mushroom to feature, all served with bread. Lines are common but service is swift.

GRÜNERLØKKA AND EASTERN OSLO
★ Mathallen Food Hall

Inspired by the food halls of continental Europe, **Mathallen** (Vulkan 5,

Fri., 9:30am-3am Sat., 9:30am-1am Sun.) brings the best of Oslo's restaurants and food shopping under one roof. The centerpiece of the emerging riverside Vulkan neighborhood, Oslo's biggest food hall is a destination in itself. At the center of the hall are large benches encouraging social interaction and sharing of dishes, while some self-contained restaurants dot the perimeter of the spacious redbrick former factory. Fresh fruit and vegetables, a fishmonger, and a butcher counter are all available inside. Note that several of the individual shops and restaurants have different opening hours to the center itself, which is entirely closed on Mondays.

Highlights inside include **Vulkanfisk** (www.vulkanfisk.no), which sells arctic cod from Tromsø, shrimp from Kirkenes, crayfish and lobster from Møre, and organic salmon from Aukra. The selection of craft beers at basement bar **Smelteverket** (www.smelteverketoslo.no) is so vast they have built Norway's longest bar to serve them from. Join the fun at the weekly pub quiz on Wednesday from 6pm, with questions given in both Norwegian and English.

Stock up on cheeses, cured meats, and other delicacies for later from the boys at **Gutta på Haugen** (www.gutta.no). They have a bigger store at St. Hanshaugen, but the selection at Mathallen is good enough to avoid an out-of-the-way trip to the 'burbs.

The mezzanine floor offers far more than a chance to take in the atmosphere and aromas from below. The menu of the day at Latin American backpacker-themed **Hitchhiker** (tel. 95 45 14 66, www.hitchhiker.no, 11am-1am Tues.-Sat., noon-10pm Sun.) presents sharing plates crammed with street food with a slight Norwegian twist. Fish tacos anyone? The restaurant slowly transforms into a bar with a late-night DJ getting the party started on Friday nights, although it's drinks only after 10pm.

CULINARY ACADEMY
(Kulinariskakademi)
During the daytime, the mezzanine plays host to a series of food classes from Oslo's **Culinary Academy** (tel. 23 23 15 80, www.kulinariskakademi.no), including wine pairing, sushi making, and sausage making. Most courses are held in Norwegian and run around 1,200kr, but classes in English are available at peak times, so check in advance.

Cafés and Light Bites
Norwegian barista ★ **Tim Wendelboe** (Grünersgate 1, tel. 40 00 40 62, 8:30am-6pm Mon.-Fri., 11am-5pm Sat.-Sun.) is the undisputed king of Nordic coffee culture, and his micro-roastery and coffee bar does a roaring trade with locals. This isn't the place to relax over a latte, as the solitary table is likely to be taken. Pop in for a black coffee brewed to order and experience a taste sensation. Not sure what to order? The menu is available in both Norwegian and English, and Tim's staff are knowledgeable bordering on obsessive about the origin of the beans. Just tell them if you prefer your

coffee with nutty, chocolaty, or fruity tones, and they'll recommend the best option for you. You're unlikely to meet the man himself, as he spends several months every year working on location with the farmers to improve the production process.

Perfect for a winter visit, the menu at **Cocoa** (Toftes gate 48, tel. 92 80 84 40, 10am-7pm daily) is packed with hot chocolate options, and, of course, they serve coffee too. Most of the light bites are made in-store by the owner, with savory pies such as spinach and feta sitting alongside sweet temptations. The retro interior is charming, but even if it's busy, you can pick up cocoa to go from the serving window.

The Grunerløkka branch of **Godt Brød** (Thorvald Meyers gate 49, tel. 23 22 90 40, 6am-6pm daily) is the best option for breakfast or a light lunch. All sandwiches are made to order, and there's a bigger range of fresh toppings and sauces, and more seating than most other cafés in Oslo. The coffee's good, too!

Traditional Scandinavian

If you need to shake off the hipster attitude of Grünerløkka and desire something more formal, **Markveien Mat & Vinhus** (Torvbakkgt 12, tel. 22 37 22 97, www.markveien.no, 4pm-1am Mon.-Sat., 275kr) is the place for you. This is the kind of warm, cozy restaurant where you make an evening of it. Fish and seafood feature strongly on the menu, with an excellent five-course set menu available for 600kr. The associated wine bar is one of Oslo's oldest, and you will be hard pressed to ignore the tantalizing range of wines on offer to accompany your meal, even if they could double the price.

Amid the thrift stores and takeaways of multicultural Grønland is the surprisingly stylish **Olympen** (Grønlandsleiret 15, tel. 24 10 19 99, www. olympen.no, noon-midnight Sun.-Mon., 11am-1am Tues.-Thurs., 11am-3am Fri., noon-3am Sat., 220kr). Reminiscent of a German *bierkeller* (basement pub), the dark wooden interior is in complete contrast to the bright and spacious rooftop terrace open during the summer months. Popular with groups, Olympen serves traditional Scandinavian fare, although the menu is often limited to one meat and two fish dishes. This is no place for vegans.

With perhaps the best view from any restaurant in Oslo, **Ekebergrestauranten** (Kongsveien 15, tel. 23 24 23 00, www.ekebergrestauranten.com, 11am-midnight Mon.-Sat., noon-10pm Sun.) is in a modernist building within the peaceful surroundings of Ekeberg Park. Prime cuts of meat or fish are served simply yet elegantly with terrific views and a direct tram link to the city. Expect to pay around 180kr for a simple lunch of cured salmon or a hamburger, while a more formal dinner will run around 285kr for your entrée.

Asian

Always a comforting sign for a sushi restaurant, **Mamo Sushi** (Helgesens gate 16, tel. 22 37 10 38, 3pm-10pm Sun.-Thurs., 3pm-11pm Fri.-Sat.,

109-195kr) attracts a lot of Japanese guests. Its popularity and relatively small interior mean booking is advisable if you want to enjoy the generous sharing plates. If you're especially hungry, start with the excellent spicy Thai soup.

For a budget option, check out the Chinese, Vietnamese, Thai, and sushi menu at the shabby yet busy **East Kitchen** (Markveien 50, tel. 22 71 96 58, 11am-10pm Mon.-Fri., noon-10pm Sat., 1pm-10pm Sun.). Their midweek lunch deal (11am-3pm) for under 100kr has to be one of the best culinary bargains in the city, and the locals know it. Head here after the lunchtime rush and you might not need much of an evening meal.

Indian

Grønland is home to a concentration of Indian restaurants, the best of which is **Punjab Tandoori** (Gronland 24, tel. 22 17 20 86, www.punjabtandoori.no, 11am-11pm daily, 110kr). The interior feels like a fast-food outlet, and you will need to listen out for your order as it's shouted from the counter. Be especially attentive when it's busy, which is most of the time given that it's one of Oslo's best-value places to eat a decent-sized meal.

Tucked away on a residential street in nearby Tøyen, **Palmyra Cafe** (Norby gata 15, www.palmyra.no, 11am-9pm daily, 110kr) is a no-frills South Indian and Sri Lankan restaurant with a focus on simple, traditional food. Don't let the school cafeteria-style plastic serving trays put you off; this is authentic and great value food from the Indian subcontinent.

Italian

For thin and crispy Italian-style pizza, look no further than **Villa Paradiso** (Olaf Ryes plass 8, tel. 22 35 40 60, www.villaparadiso.no, 8am-11pm Mon.-Fri., 10am-11pm Sat.-Sun., 181kr), even if the crusts are often a little overdone. Located on one of Grunerløkka's busiest squares, the pizzeria is always popular in the evenings, so be sure to book ahead. Walk-ins are usually possible for lunch, and takeout is always available, but orders are not accepted over the phone. The outside terrace fills up fast, but there's plenty more seating inside the warm Italian bar area.

WESTERN OSLO
Cafés and Light Bites

The airy **Cafe Rustique** (Majorstuveien 33b, tel. 22 59 35 00, 8am-6pm Mon.-Fri., 10am-6pm Sat.-Sun.) is known for its international atmosphere, but that's down to the global nature of its staff and clientele rather than the food. The much-lauded empanadas aren't worth the premium price, so save your money and stick to a croissant and coffee instead. Choose between the moody cramped interior or one of the few sidewalk tables on the street corner.

Traditional Scandinavian

It might be a little tricky to find (look for the plants!), but **Kolonihagen**

lunch at Mathallen food hall

Black, copper, and gold dominate The Thief hotel.

(Frognerveien 33, tel. 99 31 68 10, www.kolonihagen.no, 11am-11pm Mon.-Sat., 11am-5pm Sun., 279kr) is worth the effort. Set back from the street in the upscale residential neighborhood of Frogner, Kolonihagen brings the freshest Scandinavian ingredients from the farm to your plate in a relaxed rustic environment. Also available as a vegetarian version, the seasonal tasting menu is the best way to sample the taste of Kolonihagen, although taking the accompanying drink pairings will push the check over 1,100kr per head.

International

The Ivorian chef at **Café Afrikaden** (Pilestredet 75c, tel. 21 39 61 06, www.cafeafrikaden.no, 4pm-9pm Mon.-Fri., 2pm-10pm Sat., 130kr) focuses on authenticity with a rotating weekly menu. The café offers a rare chance to sample African food in Oslo. Rice and fried plantains are common accompaniments, but you might need sunglasses to protect your eyes from the vivid mismatched decor.

There are plenty of cheaper Indian restaurants in Oslo, but **Natraj Tandoori** (Bygdøy allé 8, tel. 22 44 75 33, www.natraj.no, 4pm-11pm Mon.-Sat., 3pm-10pm Sun., 199kr) serves generous flavorful portions in a colorful atmosphere that has placed it as a firm favorite among diners in western Oslo.

A great choice for those passing through Majorstuen due to its proximity to the metro station, **Café Billabong** (Bogstadveien 53, tel. 22 60 42 97, www.cafebillabong.no, 11am-1am Mon.-Thurs., 11am-3am Fri.-Sat., noon-midnight Sun., 140kr) offers a daily special on top of its vast range of pizzas, burgers, and pasta dishes. The food is nothing special, but it's filling, good value, and served quickly. As the day progresses, the atmosphere transforms from sleepy to lively as the booths become home to groups for drinking games galore.

The menu changes daily at **Krishna's Cuisine** (Sørkedalsveien 10, tel. 22 60 62 50, 11am-8pm Mon.-Fri., 11am-7pm Sat., 150kr) but is always limited to one combination of curry, soup, rice, and sides. Drinks are limited to juice, coffee, water, or lassi, a traditional Indian yogurt-based drink. Set inside a mall, this is not the place to come for a romantic dinner, but it's a great value option for vegetarians on this side of the city.

NORTHERN OSLO
Traditional Scandinavian

Traditional Norwegian food in a rustic cabin environment with sensational views across Oslo—there's not much not to like about **Frognerseteren** (Holmenkollveien 200, tel. 22 92 40 40, www.frognerseteren.no, noon-10pm Mon.-Sat., 1pm-9pm Sun., 365kr). Top quality reindeer, lamb, and local fish are served with simple accompaniments. During the daytime, the adjacent café serves a slimmer sandwich menu alongside an abundance of fresh cakes to keep hungry hikers and skiers satisfied before they continue their journey into the Nordmarka forest.

Farther down the hill, the **Holmenkollen Restaurant** (Holmenkollveien 119, tel. 22 13 92 00, www.holmenkollenrestaurant.no, noon-9pm Tues.-Sat., 1pm-7pm Sun., closed in July, 299kr) serves a Norwegian menu with the odd international twist in a traditional mountain lodge setting. The biggest pull here is not the food, but the outstanding views across the Oslofjord.

Accommodations

Recent years have seen a wave of simple budget hotels arrive in the Norwegian capital, a trend we hope to see spread to the smaller cities in due course. Chain hotels still dominate the city, though, and in some areas of central Oslo you can't walk more than a block without hitting a Thon or Scandic hotel. Thon alone boasts 16 hotels across the city.

Hostel beds are expensive in comparison to other European capitals, but availability is good. However, for not much more money you can now get motel-standard rooms in central locations, without having to share a bathroom with anyone.

DOWNTOWN
Under 500kr

Anker Hostel (Storgata 55, tel. 22 99 72 00, www.ankerhostel.no, dorm beds from 250kr pp) offers beds in a simple six- or eight-bed dormitory just across the bridge from Grünerløkka. The biggest dorms contain kitchenettes, which can prove an invaluable money-saver. Borrow a pan from reception and whip up some noodles from the budget supermarket across the street. The 24-hour reception staffed by locals is handy for late arrivals or questions about transportation. Buses and trams trundle by the entrance en route to most parts of the city.

An alternative budget option is the **Sentrum Pensjonat** (Tollbugata 8a, tel. 22 33 55 80, www.sentrumpensjonat.no, dorm beds from 290kr pp). The central location means pretty much anywhere in downtown Oslo is within a 10-minute walk. Dorm rooms are dated, the walls are salmon-pink, and noise can be an issue in this area, but that aside it's the best value accommodation in the city center. Private twin/double rooms are also available from 670kr.

500-1,000kr

The best of the recent budget bunch is the ★ **Comfort Hotel Xpress Youngstorget** (Møllergata 26, tel. 22 03 11 00, xpress.youngstorget@choice. no, 900kr), aimed squarely at hip young things. From the free coffee and fast Wi-Fi to retro arcade machines in reception, this hotel is on the stylish side of budget. The comfortable minimalist rooms with a splash of color are small, but storage isn't a problem.

The tiny rooms at **Citybox Oslo** (Prinsens gate 6, tel. 21 42 04 80, www. citybox.no, 795kr) will not please those with a lot of luggage, but they're fine for an individual or a couple traveling light. The outstanding location just a few minutes' walk from Oslo Central Station is perfect for late-night arrival. The automated reception won't please everyone, but there is usually a member of staff on call. The hostel-style social lounge with library and TVs helps to make up for the small rooms.

The outstanding value **HTL Karl Johan** (Arbeidergata 4, tel. 97 99 56 30, 799kr) has spacious rooms with LED lights and a modern TV system that you stream videos to from your tablet or laptop. A comfortable lounge fills the lobby area with friendly service from the bar at your seat. Included in the room rate is a quality breakfast but with not much variety—fine for one or two nights, but any more and you'll find yourself seeking some variety in the nearby cafés. If the hotel is full, try your luck at the almost identical **HTL Grensen** (Grensen 20, tel. 97 99 56 20, 799kr), literally around the corner.

1,000-2,000kr

Despite now being a part of the identikit Thon hotel chain, the **Hotel Bristol** (Kristian IV's gate 7, tel. 22 82 60 00, post@bristol.no, 1,645kr) retains its historic name and independent character. Sophisticated and traditional design combine with a live piano bar to provide a timeless elegance for its guests to enjoy, in both the rooms and common areas. The hotel's Winter Garden and Library Bar has a strong history in the city's cultural circles and offers freshly baked cakes and coffee daily to guests.

A good self-catering option, the popular **Oslo Korttidsutleie** apartments (Rostockgata 7, tel. 92 01 09 70, www.oslokorttidsutleie.no, from 1,200kr) at the new Barcode development get booked up fast. This will suit those who want a taste of how the other half live, with spotless modern studio and one-bedroom apartments with balcony views of the Oslo Opera House and Oslofjord.

Prices vary seasonally at the **Hotel Christiania Teater** (Stortingsgate 16, tel. 21 04 38 00, stay@christianiateater.com), but rooms with striking design and bold colors can usually be found for under 2,000kr. The original theater building dates back to 1917, and the hotel's common areas are filled with nods to Oslo's cultural history, from early performances of *Peer Gynt* to when Norwegian opera icon Kirsten Flagstad played her first major lead role. Today, the Christiania Teater puts on regular musicals, and the National Theater is merely steps away.

Sustainability is high on the agenda at the **Hotel Guldsmeden** (Parkveien 78, tel. 23 27 40 00, www.guldsmedenhotels.com, 1,495kr), with organic toiletries in all the rooms and local produce for breakfast. It has a sister hotel in Bali and it shows, with a unique combination of Balinese decor crossed with a Norwegian cabin. Most rooms contain four-poster beds and reindeer furs for a warm and welcoming stay.

Over 2,000kr

Five-star luxury doesn't come cheap, although ★ **The Thief** (Landgangen 1, tel. 24 00 40 00, www.thethief.com, 2,940kr) is named after its waterside location where thieves were executed rather than the price of its rooms. The striking black, copper, and gold lobby gives you an inkling of what to expect. The walls of the lobby are adorned with modern art from the neighboring Astrup Fearnley Museum, while tablet computers control the amenities within the contemporary luxury rooms. The buffet breakfast is outstanding, with hot options cooked to order and a fine range of fresh juices sourced from local orchards.

The **Grand Hotel** (Karl Johans gate 31, tel. 23 21 20 00, www.grand.no, 2,336kr) is a landmark hotel dating back to 1874. Dominating the city's primary plaza and overlooking the Parliament, the Grand Hotel plays host to visiting Nobel Peace Prize laureates and was the preferred haunt of Norwegian playwright Henrik Ibsen. Despite the hotel's age the rooms are surprisingly modern, with white and gold decor lending an airy feeling. Despite renovations, the character of the whole building has been preserved, and the stores out front are unable to use glaring billboards.

The crowning glory at **Hotel Continental** (Stortingsgata 24/26, tel. 22 82 40 00, www.hotelcontinental.no, 2,095-3,030kr) is the bar lounge Dagligstuen, home to one of Norway's largest private collections of Edvard Munch's work. The lounge hosts afternoon tea every Saturday. The upscale rooms are decorated in subdued tones, but only the upgraded rooms feature seating areas. If you want to spend even more money, the hotel offers packages combining lavish dinners or spa treatments, or a romantic package that features fruit, wine, room service, early check-in, and a late check-out.

For a boutique luxury experience, look no further than the seven exquisite bedrooms of **Camillas Hus** (Parkveien 31, tel. 94 85 60 15, www.

camillashus.no, 1,999kr s, 2,750kr d), located just behind the Royal Palace park and named after one of Norway's most renowned female authors, Camilla Collett. You'll feel like royalty in the individually decorated rooms in which the extravagant bathrooms are the main feature. The personal touches like fresh fruit and flowers in the bedrooms make all the difference, while a cooked-to-order hot breakfast is the icing on the cake.

GRÜNERLØKKA AND EASTERN OSLO

Because it's surprisingly bereft of accommodation options, most people interested in the Grünerløkka neighborhood simply stay downtown. One great option is the riverside ★ **PS:Hotell** (Maridalsveien 13c, tel. 23 15 65 00, www.pshotell.no, 1,250kr pp) at the heart of the emerging Vulkan district with the Mathallen food hall as its neighbor. The hotel is staffed by people who need guidance, knowledge, and experience on their way back to employment. As a result, customer service is a priority here, and any queries or problems are quickly addressed. The 31 rooms are basic (some of the double rooms actually come with bunk beds) yet with an urban style designed to appeal to a younger, socially conscious patron.

For longer stays in Oslo, do as the locals do and stay in a fashionable apartment complex. The cost-effective weekly rate at the **Downtown Apartments** (Nedre gate 8, tel. 22 60 83 00, www.dta.as) ranges from 4,704kr for a studio to 10,605kr for a four-bed option. Head farther east to Tøyen for a cheaper option at the **Oslo Hotel Apartments** (Kjølberggata 29, tel. 24 07 40 03, www.oslohotelapartments.com), which offers dorm beds from 210kr, a room in a shared apartment from 490kr, or standard double rooms from 770kr.

WESTERN OSLO

The leafy western suburbs of Oslo are dominated by apartments and guesthouses rather than hotels. One exception is the popular **Saga Hotel** (Eilert Sundts gate 39, tel. 22 55 44 90, www.sagahoteloslo.no), whose 19th-century exterior hides a cutting-edge design inside. Gold and copper tones add a sense of luxury to the 47 rooms. The hotel also operates apartments in the vicinity, just steps away from the exclusive boutiques and restaurants of Bogstadveien.

The homey feel of **Villa Frogner** (Nordraaks gate 26, tel. 22 56 19 60, 1,195kr), together with its location just steps from Vigeland Sculpture Park, draws many travelers away from downtown. A friendly host, free tea and coffee, and vintage furniture in the communal areas give this bed-and-breakfast an altogether different feel from the soulless chain hotels all too common elsewhere in Oslo, as do the individually decorated spacious rooms. There's a cheaper alternative just a few streets away at the three-room **Frogner Bed & Breakfast** (Kirkeveien 5, tel. 92 42 03 65, post@frognerbb.no, 850kr), where the small rooms are simply furnished. There's a lack of common areas and no permanent reception, so it feels more like a lodging than a commercial B&B.

Plenty of accommodation options are available through **Frogner House** (tel. 93 01 00 09, www.frognerhouse.no), a network of intimate apartments across the neighborhood. Especially good for a short stay are the apartments in the ornate former hotel at Bygdøy allé 53, where all rooms contain a kitchenette and smart TV.

NORTHERN OSLO

Leaping out of the pages of a Norwegian folk tale, the rustic **Lysebu Hotel** (Lysebuveien 12, tel. 21 51 10 00, www.lysebu.no, 1,950kr d) is possibly the finest accommodation choice in Oslo. Surrounded by forest yet just a short stroll from Oslo's T-Bane network, the hotel features a swimming pool and well-stocked wine cellar that make Lysebu a destination in itself. This is an absolutely perfect choice if you want to explore Oslo's forest and the Holmenkollen area any time of year. Designed by architect Magnus Paulsson as a monument to Danish-Norwegian cooperation during World War II, Lysebu showcases a range of art from the two countries. Combine this setting with the light, rustic bedrooms and you'd be hard-pressed to find a better venue for a romantic getaway, especially in the winter.

Few hotels in the city offer views as good as the **Scandic Holmenkollen Park** (Kongeveien 26, tel. 22 92 20 00, holmenkollenpark@scandichotels.com, 1,390kr), sandwiched between Holmenkollen and the city below. The striking contrast of the fanciful architecture resembling a Norwegian stave church with the modern ski jump is an exciting one, yet many of the hotel's 300-plus rooms are located in a far less interesting modern block. Still, for fresh air and access to Holmenkollen and Oslo's forests, this is a great choice. The hotel is extremely busy in winter, especially during major skiing events.

Primarily a conference hotel, **Thon Hotel Ullevaal** (Sognsveien 77C, tel. 22 02 80 00, ullevaalstadion@thonhotels.no, 1,116kr) is nevertheless a good choice for sports fans. The hotel is immediately adjacent to the national soccer stadium and soccer museum, and the restaurant used for breakfast comes with a view across the soccer pitch. Rooms can be picked up for under 1,000kr a night at weekends, but rates shoot sky-high when the stadium is in use.

Camping might not be your first thought when staying in a destination famed for its winter climate, but Oslo has its own year-round campground at **Bogstad Camping** (Ankerveien 117, tel. 22 51 08 00, www.bogstadcamping.no), which is close to Bogstad Manor, Holmenkollen Ski Arena, and Oslo Winter Park. Nightly camping fees start at 200kr for two people without a car, while hookups for RVs are also available amid the 800 pitches on offer. The 55 comfortable cabins range 550-1,400kr depending on size and season, while a new kitchen block is free to use for all camping guests. Although the campground is one of Norway's biggest, it rarely feels busy due to its proximity to outdoor recreation. Its neighbors include a popular lake, a golf course, and a myriad of hiking and cross-country skiing trails.

AIRPORT HOTELS

For those with an early departure or late arrival at Oslo Airport Gardermoen, a range of hotel options will meet your needs. Be aware that although cheaper than hotels downtown, all airport hotels except the Radisson and Park Inn require an expensive shuttle bus trip or an even more pricey cab. Your best option is probably to stay downtown close to Oslo Central Station.

As you would expect for an airport hotel, the staff at the **Radisson Blu Oslo Airport** (Hotellvegen, tel. 63 93 30 00, info.airport.oslo@radissonblu.com, 1,995kr) are fully knowledgeable about procedures at Oslo Airport and are only too willing to help. The food and drinks are eye-wateringly expensive but good quality. For a luxury beginning or end to your holiday this is a good pick, but if you're watching your budget try one of the cheaper alternatives outside the airport ring.

The best of the bunch is the **Comfort Hotel Runway** (Hans Gaardersvei 27, tel. 63 94 88 88, co.runway@choice.no, 799kr), where its simplicity is disguised by contemporary design features and a view of the runway, giving the impression that you're staying in a much higher quality hotel. The lobby includes a small convenience store and restaurant that provides a free breakfast or an early-bird "grab bag" from 4am.

Information and Services

VISITOR INFORMATION

For general information about attractions and things to do in Oslo and free Wi-Fi, head to the modern **Oslo Visitor Centre** (Østbanehallen, Jernbanetorget 1, tel. 81 53 05 55, www.visitoslo.com, 9am-6pm daily) near Oslo Central Station. City maps are available from most hotel receptions. If you ever get lost in Oslo, ask a local. Everyone speaks English and most are only too happy to help a tourist, especially with the confusing T-Bane system or bus routes.

POST OFFICES AND COURIER SERVICES

Posten is the national post service and handles all domestic and international mail. Many supermarkets have an in-store postal service (post i butikk), but for parcels and detailed questions, you're best to head to the main **Posten** (Klingenberggata 7, 7:30am-6pm Mon.-Fri., 10am-3pm Sat.) at Vika. If it's just a stamp you need, most souvenir shops sell them alongside postcards.

EMBASSIES AND CONSULATES

Most nations have an embassy or consulate in Oslo. Most are located in western Oslo. Be aware that most follow Norwegian holidays as well as the holidays of their own country.

The **Embassy of the United States** (Henrik Ibsens gate 45, tel. 23 96 05 55, http://norway.usembassy.gov) remains at its city center location until the lengthy move to new premises at Huseby is finally completed. The emergency hotline for U.S. citizens (tel. 21 30 85 40) deals with lost/stolen passports, crime, deaths, and contact information for health-care providers. For all other issues, an appointment must be made to visit the embassy in person. They cannot act as your travel agent, bank, interpreter, employment office, lawyer, investigator, or law enforcement agent, or assist with personal legal or medical matters, but they can advise you on where to receive help on such matters.

Similar emergency support and services are available from the **Embassy of Canada** (Wergelandsveien 7, tel. 22 99 53 00, oslo@international. gc.ca) and the **British Embassy** (Thomas Heftyes gate 8, tel. 23 13 27 00, UKinNorway@fco.gov.uk).

Australian citizens should contact the **Australian Embassy in Denmark** (tel. +45/7026 3676, http://denmark.embassy.gov.au); the Oslo Consulate closed in 2013.

INTERNET ACCESS

Wireless Internet connectivity is commonplace in Norwegian hotels, shopping centers, and cafés.

As an alternative or to surf for longer periods of time, try the main branch of the **Oslo Public Library** (Arne Garborgs plass 4, tel. 23 43 29 00, 9am-7pm Mon.-Fri., 10am-4pm Sat.). Head to the top floor for the most seats and quietest environment.

For more comprehensive business services, ask at your hotel or head to **Arctic Internet** (Jernbanetorget 1, tel. 22 17 19 40, 9am-11pm daily) on the mezzanine floor of Oslo Central Station. There you will find printers, webcams, headsets, scanners, and CD burners in addition to regular Internet terminals.

NORWEGIAN LANGUAGE COURSES

Norwegian is a language of many dialects, but the Oslo version (Eastern Norwegian) is the one considered easiest for foreigners to learn. The **University of Oslo** (www.uio.no) runs an International Summer School in Norwegian language and culture but restricts its pure language courses to students and employees. Private language schools have exploded in popularity in recent years but tend to require a commitment of at least five weeks for beginners, costing from 4,000kr.

Alfaskolen (Kongens gate 15, tel. 22 41 01 20, www.alfaskolen.no) runs an intensive summer school at 1,800kr for the first week, with discounts for extra weeks.

Undoubtedly your best financial option is to study beforehand and use your time in Oslo to put into practice what you've learned. Many enterprising Norwegians living abroad offer lessons via video chat. Because of the lower cost of living, they are able to offer lessons at far cheaper rates than can teachers needing to meet Oslo's stratospheric cost of living.

MONEY

Banking in Oslo is largely conducted digitally. Although all shops still accept cash, times are changing fast and credit cards, wireless, and mobile payments are fast replacing bills and coins. Most shops are likely to accept all international cards, although the smallest might only accept credit cards. If in doubt, it's wise to make sure you have at least some cash on you at all times.

Cash and travelers checks can be exchanged at **Forex Bank** (Jernbanetorget 1, tel. 22 17 22 65, 7am-9pm Mon.-Fri., 9am-6pm Sat., 10am-5pm Sun.) inside Oslo Central Station and is usually a better option than hunting out a bank. Many Norwegian bank branches no longer deal with cash transactions, directing you toward the ATMs. Larger branches open later include **DNB** (Karl Johans gate 27, 9am-6pm Mon.-Fri., 10am-4pm Sat.), **Nordea** (Prinsensgate 12, 9am-3pm Mon.-Fri.), and **SpareBank** (Youngstorget 5, 9am-6pm Mon.-Thurs., 9am-3pm Fri.).

Most ATMs *(minibank)* around Oslo accept international debit and credit cards and often offer a decent exchange rate, depending on your own bank's charges.

HEALTH

Many risks typically associated with traveling are minimized in Oslo. Tap water is generally drinkable.

Urgent Care

Oslo has a number of first-aid centers *(legevakt)* that act as emergency rooms. Waits can be long, but for urgent care this should be your first port of call. **Legevakt Storgata** (Storgata 40, tel. 22 11 72 96) is the main downtown center and is open 24 hours. For illnesses including fevers, vomiting, and diarrhea, the nearby **Legevakt Aker** (Trondheimsveien 235, tel. 23 48 72 00) is also an option, but opening hours are restricted (4pm-1:30am Mon.-Fri., 10am-1:30am weekends and holidays).

Pharmacies

Every shopping center will have at least one of the major pharmacy *(apotek)* chains. Boots, Apotek 1, and Vitusapotek are the main names to look out for. There are at least 10 in the vicinity of Oslo Central Station. **Vitusapotek Jernbanetorget** (Jerbanetorget 4B, tel. 23 35 81 00) is open 24 hours, as is the **Apotek1 Legevakten** (Storgata 40, tel. 22 98 87 20) at the Storgata urgent care center.

Dental Services

Dental treatment in Oslo is expensive, so much so that medical tourism to eastern Europe is big business. Nevertheless there are options should you need emergency treatment. Precious few dental centers open on Sunday, and those that do charge a premium.

The City of Oslo runs an emergency room for dental treatment that is only open on evenings and weekends. **Oslo Tannlegevakten** (Schweigaardsgate 6, tel. 22 67 30 00, 7pm-10pm Mon.-Fri., 11am-2pm and 7pm-10pm Sat.-Sun.) is on the third floor of The Gallery above Oslo Bus Terminal. Credit cards are accepted, but with rates starting at 565kr for just 10 minutes, the bill is likely to make your eyes water just as much as the treatment.

Oslo Tannlegesenter (Tordenskiolds gate 6B, tel. 22 42 49 50, www.oslotannlegesenter.no, 8am-9pm Mon.-Fri., 10am-5pm Sat.-Sun.) welcomes emergency calls, although on a Sunday you will need to call 95 36 65 28 to inquire about the availability of a dental practitioner.

Transportation

GETTING THERE
Air
OSLO AIRPORT GARDERMOEN

Although a 49-kilometer (30-mile) drive northeast of the city center, **Oslo Airport Gardermoen** (Edvard Munchs veg, Gardermoen, tel. 64 81 20 00) is the main international hub for Norway, with flights to the United States, Middle East, and Asia alongside domestic and European routes. Both international and domestic terminals have undergone a massive expansion, so congestion issues should now be a thing of the past.

To reach Oslo, choose between the nonstop 20-minute journey on the modern **Airport Express Train (Flytoget)** (www.flytoget.no, 180kr) or the 30-40-minute ride on the commuter train from **NSB** (www.nsb.no, 93kr). Both options run from approximately 5am to midnight. The express option has much more room for luggage, but the commuter service is a great budget option for those traveling light. In contrast, the **Airport Express Coach (Flybussen)** (www.flybussen.no, 150kr) is both expensive and slow. It can take up to an hour to reach the city at busy times.

OTHER AIRPORTS

Previously known as Oslo's second airport, Moss Airport Rygge ceased operations in late 2016 following the withdrawal of low-cost carrier Ryanair. The only alternative airport for Oslo is now **Sandefjord Airport Torp** (tel. 33 42 70 00, www.torp.no), approximately 110 kilometers (68 miles) south of Oslo, on the western side of the Oslofjord. Although Sandefjord Airport is commonly advertised as Oslo Torp by low-cost carriers, the compact regional airport is actually an expensive two-hour bus transfer to and from the capital. Nevertheless, it's worth considering, as bargains can be had from the United Kingdom and continental Europe.

Bus

Located at the eastern edge of downtown, **Oslo Bus Terminal** (Schweigaards gate 6-14) is the arrival point for all international bus routes. **Swebus** (www.swebus.se) runs regular coaches from Stockholm, Gothenburg, and Copenhagen, from where **Eurolines** (tel. +49/6196-2078-501, www.euro-lines.de) offers connections to Berlin, Frankfurt, and Hamburg. **Czech Transport** (tel. +420/776-677-890 Mon.-Fri., www.czech-transport.com) runs a weekly service from Prague.

When arriving at Oslo Bus Terminal, be sure to keep hold of your belongings and head straight for the neighboring Oslo Central Station. Although Oslo is generally considered to be a safe city, care should be taken inside and in the area immediately outside the bus station.

Rail

Also on the east of downtown, **Oslo Central Station** (Jernbanetorget 1, tel. 81 50 08 88, www.oslo-s.no) is linked into the European rail network via Swedish cities Gothenburg and Stockholm. Three daily trains make the four-hour journey from Gothenburg, and tickets can be booked via the Norwegian state railway company **NSB** (tel. 81 50 08 88, www.nsb.no), but to make the five-hour journey from Stockholm, you must book in advance with the Swedish state company **SJ** (tel. +46/771 757 575, www.sj.se).

If you are arriving by rail and plan to continue your journey around Norway by rail, it's worth investigating the rail passes on offer. Non-Europeans can use Eurail (www.eurail.com) and European citizens Interrail (www.interrail.eu). Both passes are particularly good value for those under 25 and for families traveling together.

Boat

In addition to the increasing numbers of cruise ships, three international ferry operators service Oslo. **DFDS** (tel. +44/330 333 0245, www.dfdssea-ways.co.uk) operates overnight boats from Copenhagen, while **Color Line** (tel. 81 00 08 11, www.colorline.no) runs a daily service to and from Kiel in northern Germany. **Stena Line** (tel. 23 17 91 30, www.stenaline.no) operates a 24-hour round-trip service to and from Fredrikshavn in northern Denmark known locally as a "booze cruise." Oslo locals take advantage of the duty-free regulations on board, often stumbling back into Oslo with crates of beer in tow.

GETTING AROUND
Public Transit

Oslo's public transit system is extensive and collectively managed under the umbrella organization **Ruter** (www.ruter.no). This means that, although the metro, tram, bus, train, and ferries are operated by different companies, there is one ticketing solution for more or less the entire network. The Ruter network extends out of Oslo and into the surrounding Akershus county.

Pay attention to the multiple zone ticketing system, although you will only need a ticket for more than one zone if you are traveling outside of Oslo.

The excellent English version of their website helps you plan your travel around the city and gives up-to-date information on fares and passes. Whichever mode of transport you choose, you in most cases need to purchase your tickets in advance and ensure they are validated or you risk a heavy fine. Ignorance is no excuse in the eyes of the Oslo public transit cops. A single fare (valid for 60 minutes including transfers on bus, metro, and tram) for one zone costs 33kr when bought in advance, with a 24-hour ticket at 90kr good value if you are planning a hectic day of sightseeing. Children under 4 travel fee, with a discount (usually 50 percent) applied for children under 16 and seniors above 67.

At almost all public transit stops you will find live information screens detailing how long you will need to wait for any particular service. These tend to be accurate, but there are paper timetables at the majority of stops too, just in case. Smoking is banned on all public transport and also at the stops. The usually shy and reserved Norwegians won't hesitate to interrupt a visitor who violates this law.

Most modes of transport are up and running by 6am through to midnight, with some bus lines running throughout the night. The rush hour in Oslo tends to be early, so you'll find public transport at its busiest before 8am and 3pm-5pm.

METRO

Oslo's metro network, known as **T-Bane** (look for the T logo), is extensive considering the compact nature of the city. The lines all converge into one tunnel that serves all six stations in the vicinity of downtown Oslo, meaning you can get onto any line from any station in the city center. Many of the lines reach out far into the surrounding suburbs and offer great connectivity into Oslo's *marka,* the forested areas that envelop the city. Line 1 serves Holmenkollen Ski Arena and passes through dense forest on its way to Frognerseteren and Nordmarka, while line 3 serves the hiking and skiing trails around Sognsvann lake. It's not uncommon for both lines to be packed with winter sports enthusiasts in the winter or locals heading into the hills for a weekend hike.

TRAM

There's a certain charm to Oslo's aging tram *(trikk)* network, which is undergoing a major renovation and expansion. New lines run along the waterfront Barcode development, with more planned in due course to fill in the gaps of the T-Bane network.

BUS

The metro and tram are usually sufficient for visitors to Oslo, but there is also an extensive network of buses that fill in the gaps, in particular to residential suburbs. Green buses are regional, whereas the red ones are local and stay within the city limits. Almost all bus routes pass through the downtown area somewhere close to Jernbanetorget square.

FERRY

Oslo's passenger ferry network provides a vital transportation link from nearby islands and peninsulas to the downtown area. But they are great use to travelers, too. A daily service runs year-round from Vippetangen serving the small islands of the inner Oslofjord. All Ruter tickets and passes are valid on these ferries, with the exception of the Bygdøy tourist ferry, which requires a separate ticket.

Taxi

There is almost never a need to take a taxi in Oslo. That's a good thing, because the cost of short trips is astronomical, with prices starting at 109kr. Expect a per-kilometer rate of around 14kr, rising to almost 20kr depending on the time of day. If you really do need a taxi, **Oslo Taxi** (tel. 22 38 80 90, www.oslotaxi.no, 24 hours) is your best bet. All their taxicabs accept major credit cards, including Diners Club and American Express.

Car Rental

All international car rental companies are represented at both Oslo Airport and in the city itself. Expect to pay around 3,000kr for a week's basic rental from the likes of **Avis** (tel. 67 25 55 10, www.avis.no) or **Hertz** (tel. 64 81 05 50, hertz.no) from Oslo Airport.

A good alternative option, **Rent-a-wreck** (www.rent-a-wreck-scandinavia.com) rents out used cars starting at 300kr per day, although they charge additional fees for extensive mileage. They have outlets at Økern (Østre Akervei 21) and Jessheim (Ringveien 31), near Oslo Airport.

Oslofjord

A world away from the dramatic western Norwegian fjords, the Oslofjord is nevertheless a vast expanse of water stretching over 80 kilometers (50 miles) south from the Norwegian capital. Almost half of Norway's population lives within a one-hour drive from the fjord, so there's plenty to see along the shoreline, from idyllic islands, skerries, and lighthouses to major commercial centers of trade and industry.

The quaint fishing village Drøbak marks the entrance to the Inner Oslofjord, where the waterway narrows, the population increases, and the islands become increasingly inhabited. Seagulls, oystercatchers, terns, and geese are commonly sighted along these narrow waters.

The region is one of Norway's warmest, and on summer days Oslo's residents head south and locals dash to their boats to make the most of the sunshine. The agreeable climate has attracted settlers since the days of the Stone Age and Bronze Age, so it's no surprise that some of the world's best

preserved Viking ships were discovered on these shores. The fjord was a strategically important waterway in World War II, and as such historical monuments and former military installations are commonplace.

A day trip to one of these Oslofjord destinations is a great way to break up a few days in Oslo.

DRØBAK

Largely unheard of by tourists, this quaint fjordside town at the narrowest point of the Oslofjord is one of the most popular day trips taken by residents of Oslo on a warm summer day. The big draw of Drøbak is its beaches and gentle waterside walks, while the lively harbor is busy with boat traffic, due to the many nearby islands and plentiful stocks of cod, coalfish, pollock, ling, haddock, and mussels. In the 19th century, when the inner Oslofjord used to freeze over, Drøbak acted as the winter harbor for Oslo.

Drøbak is just a one-hour bus ride or 40-minute drive from Oslo, or accessible via a sightseeing boat during the summer, so a last-minute decision to travel here is possible.

OSCARSBORG FORTRESS
(Oscarsborg festning)

Strategically located on an island in the narrowest part of the Oslofjord, the horseshoe-shaped **Oscarsborg Fortress** (Søndre Kaholmen, tel. 64 90 41 61) is best known for defeating the German cruiser *Blücher,* which still remains at the bottom of the fjord, during World War II. Visitors can enjoy a small museum, traditional smithy, art exhibition, marina, a marked trail, and a café. Opening hours vary throughout the year but are typically 10am-3pm for the museum and 11am-9pm for the café. Outside of high season (June-Aug.), it's best to bring your own food just in case the café is closed, or call in advance to check the hours.

The fortress can only be reached by boat, which runs daily year-round from Sundbrygga pier at the town harbor, at a cost of 100kr round-trip (admission is included). Journeys begin at 7am and run approximately hourly through to 11pm, but do check the schedules in advance, especially outside the summer season.

DRØBAK AQUARIUM
(Drøbak Akvarium)

Built by the local boat society, **Drøbak Aquarium** (Havnegata 4, tel. 91 10 84 20, www.drobakakvarium.no, 10am-4pm daily, 60kr) is intended to recreate the waters of the Oslofjord for enjoyment and education. Local fishers have filled the aquarium with lobsters, codfish, sea porcupines, and flounders, all sustained by a constant stream of salt water pumped in from the fjord.

TOWN CENTER

The protected status of the small town center helps to preserve its traditional 19th-century look and feel. Numerous art galleries and sidewalk cafés help to create an atmosphere that's more continental Europe than Norway.

The gallery at the **Newspaper Cartoonists' House (Avistegnernes Hus)** (Lindtrupbakken 1, tel. 66 93 66 32, www.avistegnerneshus.no, noon-4pm Tues.-Sun., 30kr) is a tribute to the artistry of comedic journalism and the universal freedom of expression. The Cartoonists' House is more than just a gallery. It offers free accommodations and workspace for persecuted newspaper cartoonists from all over the world, once they are accepted as political refugees into Norway. Exhibitions change regularly, and a wide selection of illustrated books are available for purchase.

Experience a Scandinavian Christmas in the middle of the summer at **Tregaarden's Christmas House (Tregaardens Julehus)** (Havnebakken 6, tel. 64 93 41 78, www.julehus.no, 10am-5pm Mon.-Fri., 10am-3pm Sat. Jan.-May; 10am-5pm Mon.-Fri., 10am-3pm Sat., noon-4pm Sun. June-Oct.; 10am-5pm Mon.-Fri., 10am-4pm Sat., noon-4pm Sun. Nov., 10am-8pm Mon.-Fri., 10am-4pm Sat., noon-4pm Sun. Dec.). While the ground floor of the spectacular former chapel building sells traditional Scandinavian Christmas decorations from candles to stockings, the top floor doubles as Santa's Post Office, from where you can arrange for postcards to be sent out during December.

Food and Accommodations

Enjoy lunch amid the bustling harbor atmosphere at **Skipperstuen** (Havnebakken 11, tel. 64 93 07 03, noon-10pm Mon.-Sat., 1pm-8pm Sun.), which is one of Norway's few restaurants with more seating outdoors than in. Unsurprisingly the catch of the day comes highly recommended. Before 4pm, this is served together with bread and aioli for 235kr. The atmosphere turns a touch more formal for the evening service, when more extravagant mains run up to 350kr. If you just want to graze in the afternoon sun, pick up some olives, cured meats, or cheese from the snack menu.

Spanish omelets, topped focaccia breads, and seafood tapas are among the excellent choices at the informal **Galleri Cafe Teskje** (Niels Carlsensgate 7, tel. 64 93 09 91, www.teskje.no, 10am-5pm Tues.-Sat., noon-5pm Sun.), midway along a charming street lined with galleries and boutiques. The neighboring **Kumlegaarden** (Niels Carlsensgate 11, tel. 64 93 89 90, www. kumlegaarden.no, 11:30am-8pm Mon., 11:30am-10pm Tues.-Sat., 1pm-8pm Sun., 245kr) is set inside two of Drøbak's oldest timber buildings. A raw claystone fireplace tops off a remarkable interior strewn with trinkets and flowers that will keep you occupied until the food arrives. Expect traditional Norwegian fare, generally with a choice of beef, game, or fish. Saturdays aside, lunchtime tends to be much quieter, whereas reservations for dinner are recommended throughout the week.

Accommodation options are limited, but the 28-room **Reenskaug Hotel** (Storgata 32, tel. 64 98 92 00, www.reenskaug.no, 1,590kr d) would not be out of place in the capital. Rooms are individually decorated, so it's pot luck whether you'll end up with traditional elegance or sleek modern, but all come with a pod coffee maker, flatscreen TV, and a private bathroom. The comfortable outdoor terrace helps to make this historical hotel a great choice in which to spend a day away from the capital.

Information and Services

The harborside **Drøbak Tourist Information** (tel. 64 93 50 87, 8:30am-4pm Mon.-Fri., 10am-2pm Sat.-Sun.) will help you orient yourself, suggest hikes, and confirm return transport options to Oslo. Follow signs for Drøbak Aquarium to find the office.

Getting There

Drøbak is 39 kilometers (24 miles) south of central Oslo along the main E6 highway. If making the 40-minute drive, exit the E6 onto Rv23 and follow the signs for Drøbak. Parking is free for four hours at the AMFI shopping mall, a 30-minute walk from the harbor. Street parking costs 33kr per hour (free 5pm-8am).

Public bus route 500 departs Oslo Bus Terminal every half hour throughout the day. The one-hour journey requires a two-zone ticket (52kr advance, 70kr on board), which is not covered by the Oslo Pass or the regular public transit pass, unless you specifically bought a zone extension.

FREDRIKSTAD

An easy day trip from Oslo thanks to fast rail and bus links, the otherwise ordinary Fredrikstad is worth a look because of its remarkable Old Town. The fortified streets drip character from every corner, and even though many of the old buildings now house boutiques and cafés, it's all been done with a sense of dignity.

Founded in 1567 by Denmark-Norway King Fredrik II as a trading post between the European mainland and western Scandinavia, Fredrikstad was fortified to protect itself from the risk of Swedish invasion. Burned to the ground twice, the fortifications were strengthened with the distinctive jagged moat to a point when Fredrikstad became the best protected city in Norway. Because the modern city grew up on the other side of the Glomma river, the Old Town has been left largely intact and its 17th-century character preserved.

This is Østfold, the smallest and least mountainous of Norway's counties. The flat meadows, forest, and scenic farm buildings mark the transition to the south of Sweden. Traces of habitation dating back 8,000 years can be found across the county. With more time, explore the historical monuments from the Stone, Bronze, and Iron Ages along the Rv110 between Fredrikstad and Skjeberg, also known as the **Ancient Road (Oldtidsveien)**. Burial mounds, fortified hamlets, and rock carvings are some of the highlights. Pick up an information leaflet from the tourist information center in Fredrikstad to explore this further.

Fredrikstad's Old Town is one of Norway's best.

OLD TOWN

There's precious little to see in the modern downtown district, so visitors should waste no time in heading straight for the **Old Town (Gamle Fredrikstad)**, which requires a pleasant ferry ride across the river. From the train station, turn left and continue on down to the river bank. Pick up the compact free-of-charge **City Ferry (Byferga)**, a passenger service that runs between here and the Old Town plus a couple of suburbs throughout the day. The crossing to the Old Town takes just a couple of minutes, or you can stay on the ferry for a 30-minute tour of the river and Fredrikstad's suburbs.

Simply soaking up the atmosphere is a good use of time here, as is a ramble along the grassy embankments of the perimeter. But there are plenty of sights on this easy-to-navigate grid system of cobbled streets, if you know where to look. Head to the southern end of the district (turn right from the ferry) to see the skeletons found buried under the city hospital and now on display at **Fredrikstad Museum** (Tøihusgaten 41, tel. 69 11 56 50, noon-4pm daily, 75kr). The small museum won't take up too much of your time, but make sure to ask about some of the area's best preserved buildings, such as the convict prison and stone storehouse.

Continue your tour of Fredrikstad's history at the well-preserved embankments, turrets, and stone walls of **Kongsten Fort** (tel. 81 57 04 00, grounds always open), standing guard on a gentle hill behind the Old Town. Pick up a map to follow a self-guided tour, or just explore the pleasant grounds by yourself and let your mind wander to a time long forgotten. Alternatively, do as the locals do—bring a picnic and just relax.

A curious addition to the Old Town's attractions, the **Model Railway Center (Gamlebyen Modelljernbanesenter)** (Voldgaten 8, tel. 90 50 98 74, www.gbmj.no, 11am-4pm Mon.-Sat., noon-4pm Sun. mid-June to mid-Aug., noon-4pm Sat.-Sun. mid-Aug. to mid-June, 40kr) is a must for kids, as well as adults with even a passing interest in the railroad. Model trains run between different rooms, each with its own landscape. The attention to detail in the scenes is stunning, from people arguing in the streets to an almost-hidden couple sunbathing in the forest. Kids can control a small track themselves, while adults may feel inspired to dig out their dusty old train sets when they hear the entire center was the vision of just one man.

Food and Accommodations

OLD TOWN

A little bit of everything is on offer at the often-busy **MorMors** (Rådhusgaten 18a, tel. 69 32 16 60, 11am-5pm Mon.-Fri., 11am-6pm Sat., noon-5pm Sun.) at the heart of Fredrikstad's Old Town. Make the most of finding a table and order a heavy slice of homemade cake just like the ones your grandmother used to bake. Alternatively, grab a focaccia or light sandwich to go, then find a space on the curb outside.

The most distinctive hotel in the entire city, ★ **Gamlebyen Hotell** (Voldportgaten 72, tel. 40 05 39 09, www.gamlebyenhotell.no, 1,190kr s,

1,490kr d) is the only accommodation located within the atmospheric Old Town. Unlike the streets outside, the interior has been thoroughly modernized, with a touch of sophistication and more than a nod to the past. White wood dominates the interior, and the 15 bright rooms are individually decorated. No breakfast is included, but a discounted deal is available with the adjacent café.

The cheapest accommodation in town is hidden away behind the Old Town. **Fredrikstad Motel & Camping** (Torsnesveien 16/18, tel. 99 22 19 99, www.fredrikstadmotel.no) offers basic double motel rooms from 550kr, but the higher-quality cabins feel more like hotel rooms. They range from 850kr for a two-bed option up to 1,250kr for a cabin that sleeps up to six. Pitches for tents (150kr) and campervans (250kr) are available, with power hookups a further 50kr. Wi-Fi is available throughout, and access to the basic kitchen and bathroom facilities is included in camping rates.

CENTRAL FREDRIKSTAD

While there are few sights in the modern district, central Fredrikstad is awash with quality food and accommodation choices. Head west toward the river for the best-quality eateries or into the pedestrianized shopping streets for quick bites.

There's little argument between locals about the best restaurant in Fredrikstad. Advance booking is a must to secure a table at **Slippen** (Verkstedveien 12, tel. 99 46 99 88, www.restaurantslippen.no, 11am-10pm Tues.-Fri., noon-10pm Sat., 2pm-8pm Sun., 295kr). Outstanding presentation adds a modern twist to the classic Norwegian dishes of stockfish, fried sea trout, and oven-baked cod. Head there before 4pm to enjoy the lighter lunch menu for under 200kr.

There's no doubt **Hotel Victoria** (Turngata 3, tel. 69 38 58 00, www.hotel-victoria.no, 895kr) has seen better days, but nevertheless it offers the most budget-friendly hotel accommodations in central Fredrikstad. The decor shoots for English country elegance but ends up more like your grandmother's garish living room. Breakfast is included in all room rates.

The pick of the chain hotels is **Quality Hotel Fredrikstad** (Nygata 2-6, tel. 69 39 30 00, q.fredrikstad@choice.no, 1,195kr), the most modern hotel in the city by quite a distance. Just half a mile from the train station, the hotel's 172 modern but boxy rooms are brightened up by large windows and a fjord-inspired color scheme. A filling breakfast buffet is served until 10am, 11am on weekends.

Information and Services

It might seem sensible to house the **Fredrikstad Tourist Office** (Kirkegaten 31B, tel. 69 30 46 00, 9am-4pm Mon.-Fri.) in the Old Town, but by the time you've reached it most of your questions (where is the Old Town and how do I get there?) will have been answered. It's also strange to find a tourist information center closed on Saturday.

Getting There

Fredrikstad is located on the eastern side of the Oslofjord close to the Swedish border. By car, the 93-kilometer (58-mile) drive along the E6 should take just over one hour.

NSB (www.nsb.no) trains run hourly from Oslo Central Station to Fredrikstad throughout the day. Look for trains marked Halden or Göteborg, all of which should stop at Fredrikstad. The scenic one-hour journey costs 215kr. Alternatively, a **TIMEkspressen** (www.nettbuss.no) express bus service leaves Oslo Bus Terminal on the hour. A ticket for the 80-minute journey costs around 200kr.

Getting Around

Other than the small passenger ferry linking the Old Town to the rest of Fredrikstad, day visitors should be able to get around comfortably on foot. Otherwise, local company **Østfold Kollektivtrafikk** (tel. 69 12 54 70, www. ostfold-kollektiv.no) runs bus routes around the city and to nearby towns around the region. Single tickets cost 40kr.

TØNSBERG

Founded by the Vikings and one of Norway's most important cities in the Middle Ages, Tønsberg lays claim to be the country's oldest city. Although Tønsberg is overlooked by many international travelers, Viking burial mounds and church ruins draw in large numbers of domestic visitors, especially during the summer months when the Oslofjord is blessed with Norway's warmest climate.

For international visitors, Tønsberg makes a curious day trip of history and culture or an excellent overnight stop on a journey farther south. It is the starting point of the **Vestfold Viking Trail,** a series of ancient settlements and burial mounds from the Viking Age dotted along the coastline.

Tønsberg Wharf

Start your exploration at **Tønsberg Wharf (Tønsberg Brygge)**, the focal point of the city for more than 1,000 years. Several wooden trading warehouses from the early 19th century still stand, reminiscent of Bergen's more famous wharf. It was here that the economy of Tønsberg developed, while today the pier is noted for its restaurants and nightlife just as much as its guest marina. The pedestrian bridge across the canal is opened five times daily to allow taller ships to enter the city's main harbor.

SAGA OSEBERG

One of the most famous Viking finds in Norway took place near Tønsberg, when in 1904 the small *Oseberg* ship was discovered in a burial mound. Although the original 9th-century vessel is on display in Oslo's Viking Ship Museum, the **Saga Oseberg** (Ollebukta 3, osebergvikingskip.no) is a full-scale copy of the ship built to the original specifications and moored in the harbor just a short stroll south of Tønsberg wharf. Previous attempts to reconstruct the ship failed, including one that capsized just 20 seconds into its maiden voyage. The vessel is only taken out of its mooring for special events and research.

SLOTTSFJELL MUSEUM

Although parts of the city and its surroundings are one big museum, the **Slottsfjell Museum** (Farmannsveien 30, tel. 33 31 29 19, www.slottsfjells-museet.no, 11am-4pm Tues.-Sun., 70kr) adds some context to what you are seeing. The museum is constantly growing, with an ambition to become a medieval museum of international interest. The biggest draw is the *Klåstad* Viking ship, the only ship from the nearby finds on display outside Oslo. Following the success of the *Oseberg* replica, plans are now underway to build a new version of the *Klåstad* ship.

Immediately above the museum is the strongest pointer to Tønsberg's importance in the Middle Ages. Ruins of a 12th-century church and fortress, part of the former Royal Residence, are spread across the top of the small mountain **Slottsfjellet**. The **Slottsfjelltårnet** stone tower was erected in 1888 to celebrate the city's 1,000-year anniversary. Climb to the viewpoint for a 360-degree view of the city and fjord.

HAUGAR VESTFOLD ART MUSEUM

The star attraction at the **Haugar Vestfold Art Museum (Haugar Vestfold Kunstmuseum)** (Gråbrødregaten 17, tel. 33 30 76 70, www.haugar.com, 11am-5pm Mon.-Fri., noon-5pm Sat.-Sun. June-Aug.; 11am-4pm Tues.-Fri., noon-5pm Sat.-Sun. Sept.-May, 70kr) is the Andy Warhol paintings that were inspired by Edvard Munch's *The Scream*. Warhol's portrait of Queen Sonja is also on loan from Oslo's National Museum, so that all of Warhol's Norway-inspired work can be viewed in one location. Every Tuesday from September to May, entrance is free.

TOURS

Explore the sun-drenched archipelago to the east of Tønsberg with a summer boat trip to **Østre Bolærne** island.

From mid-June to mid-August, the **MS *Viksfjord*** (tel. 95 03 57 51, www.msviksfjord.no) leaves the Fiskebrygga quayside (a 15-minute walk from Tønsberg Wharf) at 10am daily. Stay on the boat's sun-trap rooftop terrace for a relaxing 2.5-hour cruise around the archipelago, or choose to stay on Østre Bolærne and pick up the return trip at 3:30pm or 5:40pm. The round-trip costs 250kr, or 200kr if you stay on the boat for the immediate return. Family tickets (two adults and up to three children under 16) are great value at 490kr/440kr. In the shoulder seasons (mid-May to mid-June and mid-Aug. to mid-Sept.), round-trips (no stay on the island) run at 10am and 2pm Saturday-Sunday, and 5pm Friday.

Around 3.2 kilometers (two miles) southeast of the island is the famous **Fulehuk Lighthouse (Fulehuk fyr)** (www.fulehuk.no), originally built as a stone tower in 1821. Residential buildings, a boathouse, and a steel fog bell were added some years later to help warn incoming ships of the archipelago. Today the lighthouse is used for company banquets and private celebrations, and can be seen from the cruise.

HIKING

Salty sea air, all manner of birdlife, and a glittering watery horizon are just some of the reasons for seeking out the coastal paths in and around Tønsberg. For an easy introduction to the region's hiking possibilities, explore the **Ilene Nature Reserve (Ilene Naturreservat)** northwest of the city. The 7.4-kilometer (4.6-mile) round-trip family-friendly trail signed from the wharf is lined with bird-watching stations and quiet spots for a picnic. Ask at Tønsberg Tourist Information for maps and suggested trails on the pretty coastal paths of Nøtterøy island, across the water from Tønsberg.

Entertainment and Events

Every year in early June, thousands of people flock to the top of Slottsfjellet to enjoy the pageantry of the **Tønsberg Medieval Festival (Tønsberg Middelalderfestival)** (www.tonsbergmiddelalderfestival.no, 400kr). The family-friendly daytime activities include juggling, theater, live music, and jousting tournaments, before the attention turns to an adults-only medieval banquet in the evening. Cheaper day-only tickets are available alongside a pass for the entire weekend.

At the height of summer in mid-July, **Slottsfjellfestivalen** (www.slottsfjell.no, 2,500kr) music festival welcomes a primarily Norwegian lineup of contemporary artists to the hilltop over the course of four days. The event is best known for Kastellnatt, its subterranean warehouse after-party. Despite the central location, camping is available, as the thousands of visitors far

OSLOFJORD

outstrip the number of hotel beds available in the city. Day tickets and after-party-only tickets are available alongside festival passes.

Food

The city's best restaurants are clustered together on Tønsberg Wharf. One of the longest-running is **Esmeralda** (Nedre Langgate 26c, tel. 33 31 91 91, 11am-2am Mon.-Sat., noon-11pm Sun., 199-329kr), where you can expect to enjoy excellent thin-crust pizza or fresh fish with colorful crispy vegetables while you watch the world go by from the outdoor terrace.

Stop by **The Sense** (Nedre Langgate 18, tel. 45 96 40 00, 3pm-10pm Mon.-Thurs., 3pm-2am Fri., noon-2am Sat., noon-11pm Sun., 199-297kr) for an Asian-inspired meal that still utilizes the freshest local ingredients. Light dishes of chicken satay and salmon salad are packed with flavor but won't fill you up. Grab a generous bowl of mussels for the table to ensure you leave satisfied. The modern restaurant's terrace tends to have more availability than the more traditional restaurants farther along the wharf.

For a morning pick-me-up, call in to **Bare Barista** (Øvre langgate 44, tel. 48 89 98 36, 8am-6pm Mon.-Fri., 9am-5pm Sat., 10am-5pm Sun.), a few streets back from the wharf. Although the focus is on the quality of the espresso, light sandwiches and sweet snacks are available to enjoy in the spacious backyard.

Accommodations

Modern chain hotels dominate the compact central area near the wharf, so for something with a bit more character or less expensive you'll need to look farther afield.

One exception lies at the foot of the city's hilltop near the railway station. The friendly hostess at **Tønsberg Vandrerhjem** (Dronning Blancas gate 22, tel. 33 31 21 75, 895kr d) runs a charming B&B standard hostel that books up fast with repeat visitors during the summer months. The 24 hotel-standard rooms are tight but tastefully decorated in a traditional Scandinavian style. The more spacious family rooms with bunk beds that sleep six are great value at 2,300kr, while pancakes for breakfast are a nice unexpected touch.

A five-minute walk east of the rail station is the grand **Wilhelmsen House** (Halfdan Wilhelmsens Allé 22, tel. 97 13 50 00, www.wh.no, 1,495kr d), named after the wealthy Wilhelmsen family whose international shipping empire began in the city. Light brown and beige dominate the 49 modern rooms, the biggest of which come with a well-equipped kitchenette. The luxury Jensen beds, down duvets, and oversize flatscreen TVs are some of the reasons this independent hotel has made such an impact since opening in 2015. Substantial discounts are available outside of high season.

Across the bridge on Nøtterøy island, the maritime-themed **Active Hotel** (Stalsbergveien 5, tel. 33 34 59 10, www.activehotel.no, 795kr s, 895kr d) includes free entry to the neighboring fitness center and Badeland water park for all its guests. Rooms are simply furnished and compact, but all come with private bath. A basic breakfast buffet is available for 100kr, while baguettes and salads can be bought from reception throughout the day.

Information and Services

Located inside City Hall (Rådhuset), **Tønsberg Tourist Information** (Tollbodgaten 22, tel. 33 34 80 00, 8am-3pm Mon.-Fri. year-round, 8am-3pm Sat.-Sun. mid-June to mid-Aug.) offers hiking maps, boat tour timetables, and information on small local events and markets.

Getting There

Tønsberg is a 103-kilometer (64-mile) drive south of Oslo down the E18 on the western side of the Oslofjord. **NSB** (tel. 81 50 08 88, www.nsb.no) runs an hourly regional train service from Oslo Central Station to Larvik that calls at Tønsberg. A single ticket for the 80-minute journey costs 244kr.

The city is close to **Sandefjord Airport Torp** (Torpveien 130, Sandefjord, tel. 33 42 70 00, www.torp.no), a small regional airport with Widerøe routes to Bergen and Trondheim, alongside many routes to the United Kingdom, Spain, and Poland on European budget carriers. Take the free shuttle bus between the airport and Torp railway station, which is just a 15-minute train ride (50kr) away from Tønsberg with an hourly service for much of the day.

Lillehammer

Decades before the 1994 Winter Olympics put Lillehammer on the map, this small Norwegian city and its surrounding valleys had long been a destination for winter sports fanatics. Northern Europe's highest mountain, biggest lake, and a plethora of national parks are all within range of Lillehammer.

When the city was declared host of the Olympic Games, the world checked a map. Never before had a Winter Olympics been held somewhere so small—its population is a shade over 25,000—so the city's infrastructure received substantial investment. The successful event and subsequent boost in visitors has benefited the city and the region's ski resorts ever since, and so it is much better equipped to welcome visitors than almost all other Norwegian cities of its size.

As the journey by train or car takes more than two hours, a day trip while not impossible is not advised. It's better to plan an overnight stop.

CLIMATE

Most major Norwegian cities hug the coastline for a milder climate and access to plentiful fishing grounds. Although built on the shores of the 365-square-kilometer (141-square-mile) Lake Mjøsa, Lillehammer is far inland, which has a major impact on the town's climate.

From mid-November to mid-March temperatures will likely be at or below freezing, and snow is expected. While summer days can reach a pleasant 15-20°C (59-68°F) or even higher, May to September is the wettest time of year.

ORIENTATION

Despite its status as a sporting capital, central Lillehammer is ultra-compact. The majority of shops and central attractions are located on or just off **Storgata,** which is just minutes from the railway station and bus terminal. The Maihaugen open-air museum, the Olympic Museum, and the Olympic Park are all a 15- to 20-minute walk east of the central area, but the steep hill on the way surprises many who've only glanced at a map. Buses and taxis are available.

SIGHTS
Maihaugen

Open-air museums are commonplace throughout Norway, but Lillehammer's **Maihaugen** (Maihaugvegen 1, tel. 61 28 89 00, www.maihaugen.no, 10am-5pm daily June-Aug., 11am-4pm Tues.-Sun. Sept.-May, 170kr summer, 130kr rest of year) is one of the best. Set on the hillside overlooking the city, the museum is split into three sections.

Follow the paved trail around the log cabins to find the first section, a village of three rural farms presented as they would have been in the 18th and 19th centuries. During the summer, the village is brought to life with actors playing the parts of farmers, maidens, and even the local schoolteacher.

The second section, the show town, is modeled on Lillehammer at the turn of the 20th century, so much so that many of the houses were actually moved piece by piece from the town itself. The best of those, Olsengården, housed three generations of craftsmen with hens and rabbits in the backyard.

Check out the original steam locomotive before wandering through the third section, a residential area that shows how quickly the standard of living developed during the 20th century. Typical Norwegian houses of all shapes and sizes can be found here, including a prefabricated single-story "future house" developed by Norwegian corporate giant Telenor.

Make time to visit the indoor exhibitions, including the dental office of Anders Sandvig (featuring an 1850s dentist chair and drill) and a unique range of carved folk art collected from across the Gudbrandsdalen valley. Finally, the gift shop at Maihaugen is one of Norway's best. Colorful memorabilia from the Olympic Museum sits alongside ceramics, glass, knitwear, and local crafts.

Norwegian Olympic Museum
(Norges Olympiske Museum)

The highlight of any visit to Lillehammer, at least for non-skiers, is the **Norwegian Olympic Museum** (Maihaugveien 1, tel. 61 28 89 00, http://

85

Rather than focus on the 1994 Games, the underground exhibits document the history of the global Olympic movement, both summer and winter, from ancient times through to the present day. Video installations will help you recall unforgettable moments, record-breaking performances, and inspiring opening ceremonies from around the world. Half of the museum is dedicated to Norway's Olympic history. Media coverage from Lillehammer 1994 and Oslo 1952 and a biathlon simulator are some of the highlights for non-Norwegians.

LILLEHAMMER

Olympic Park
(Olympiaparken)

Since the Olympic Museum relocated to Maihaugen, visitor numbers to the **Olympic Park** (Sigrid Undsets vei, www.olympiaparken.no) have dropped, but it's still worth a visit for sports fans. This compact site hosted the majority of events during the 1994 Games, including ice hockey, ski jumping, and the memorable opening ceremony.

On a clear day, climb the steps at **Lillehammer Ski Jumping Arena (Lysgårdsbakkene)** (9am-7pm daily mid-June to mid-Aug., 9am-4pm daily mid-May to mid-June and mid-Aug. to early Sept., 25kr) or take the chair lift (additional 35kr) for a clear view across the city and Lake Mjøsa. Even in the snow-free months of summer, serious jumpers still practice on the hill thanks to the artificial surface laid a few years ago.

Lillehammer Art Gallery
(Lillehammer Kunstmuseum)

Art meets architecture on the glistening silver-blue facade of the

ski jump in Lillehammer's Olympic Park

Weidemann Gallery at the **Lillehammer Art Museum** (Stortorget 2, tel. 61 05 44 60, www.lillehammerartmuseum.com, 11am-5pm daily late June to mid-Aug., 11am-4pm Tues.-Sun. mid-Aug. to late June, 100kr). The new addition was a collaboration between leading architecture firm Snøhetta and legendary Bergen-born artist Bård Breivik, who sadly passed away weeks before the project's opening in 2016. He was also responsible for the tranquil sculpture garden with stone and running water that links the museum's buildings.

Three private collectors donated the core of the gallery's permanent collection of 19th-century Norwegian art, which has been supplemented in recent years by the purchase of more contemporary artworks. New temporary exhibitions and retrospectives are introduced quarterly.

Family Attractions
HUNDERFOSSEN FAMILY PARK
Discover Norwegian fairy tales at the **Hunderfossen Family Park** (tel. 61 27 55 30, www.hunderfossen.no, 385kr), which is one of Norway's best family destinations despite its short summer season (mid-June to mid-Aug.). In the land guarded by a 46-foot-high troll, your family will meet Norwegian princes and princesses as you create your very own fairy-tale experience based around Norwegian folk tales.

Younger children are catered to with an indoor play center, boat pool, and splash pool, while rollercoasters will keep bigger kids amused. The five-minute ride on the simulated rapids is a must-do, but be prepared to get wet! The park is a 16-kilometer (10-mile) drive north of Lillehammer but is accessible by train or a free bus from central Lillehammer.

LILLEPUTTHAMMER
On the opposite side of the Gudbrandsdalslågen river from the Hunderfossen Family Park lies an attraction suited for younger children. At the center of **Lilleputthammer** (Hundervegen 41, tel. 61 28 55 00, www.lilleputthammer.no) is a miniaturized version of Lillehammer's main street, Storgata. The surrounding adventure park with electric-powered cars, a mini-rollercoaster, playgrounds, and colorful characters is best suited for children under 8, while the new climbing frames and zip lines of Olas klatrepark will keep children up to 12 occupied. Opening hours and prices vary wildly during the short opening season. Expect the longest hours (9am-8pm daily) but the longest queues and highest prices (314kr) throughout July. Late June and early August (10am-6pm daily, 249kr) are more reasonable, and the park is open weekends in early June and Saturdays from mid-August through September (10am-5pm Sat.-Sun., 199kr). Children under 6 receive discounted entry, while children under 3 go free. A free shuttle bus runs from Lillehammer throughout high season.

LILLEHAMMER

Olympic Bob and Luge Track

Complete the Lillehammer Olympic experience at the **Olympic Bob and Luge Track** (Hunderfossvegen 680, tel. 61 05 42 00, www.olympiaparken. no), next to Hunderfossen Family Park, 16 kilometers (10 miles) north of Lillehammer. The center offers varying experiences depending on season, using Scandinavia's only artificially frozen bobsled and luge track. Try the four-man bobsled to reach speeds of up to 120 kph (75 mph) and 5G force, or the skeleton sled, where your nose hovers barely an inch above the ice. Check the calendar in advance and book ahead to avoid disappointment, as only a limited number of runs are possible each day.

During the summer, a wheelbob (wheeled bobsled) run costs 250kr per person and is available 10am-5pm daily throughout July. The track also opens most weekends in May, June, and August. Winter opening depends on events but is typically 3pm-8pm Wednesday and noon-5pm Saturday. Bobrafting (on a rubber bobsled) costs 250kr per person, while taxibob (on an actual bobsled) or skeleton (2 runs) costs around 1,000kr per person. All bobsleds are piloted by experienced pros. A short movie of your ride can be purchased for 150kr.

Hafjell Ski & Bike Resort

One of Norway's major ski centers, **Hafjell** (Hundervegen 122-124, Hafjell, tel. 61 28 55 50, info@hafjell.no, Dec. to mid-Apr.) is just 16 kilometers (10 miles) north of Lillehammer close to the Bob and Luge Track and Hunderfossen Family Park, and linked by regular shuttle buses throughout the season. The resort is known for its Olympic-standard slopes, but it has a vast range of gentler slopes (11 blue, 10 green), seven slopes dedicated to children, plus four different terrain parks. Hafjell is also the starting point for an incredible 300 kilometers (186 miles) of prepared cross-country trails. A day's lift pass costs 405kr, with big discounts for longer stays or

Hafjell ski resort is within easy reach of Lillehammer.

evening skiing. Rental gear varies 325-445kr depending on standard, with a complete cross-country package available for 200kr.

Winter sports lovers are spoiled for choice in the Lillehammer region. Hafjell lift passes are also valid at nearby **Kvitfjell** (Fåvang, www.kvitfjell. no), 30 kilometers (18.5 miles) north of Hafjell, built specifically for the Olympics. The resort tends to attract the more serious skier.

During the summer, Hafjell is transformed into one of Norway's most challenging mountain bike parks. Open from late June, **Hafjell Bike Park** (10am-5pm Thurs.-Sun. late June to Aug., 10am-5pm Sat.-Sun. Sept.) consists of three expert-level forest trails with large step-downs and gap jumps galore, plus 11 other trails of varying difficulty. The easiest is suitable for families. A day's lift pass costs 305kr, and pro bikes can be rented for 275-795kr.

Spectator Sports

Major national and international winter sports events take place in and around Lillehammer from December to April. Check in advance because attractions, hotels, and restaurants will be overrun when the world's skiers come to town. Grabbing a ticket for a live ski jumping or biathlon event adds a truly different sporting experience to your trip. The best place to discover upcoming international events is the **International Ski Federation** (www. fis-ski.com), while **Lillehammer Tourist Information** (Jernbanetorget 2, tel. 61 28 98 00) will be up to speed on the domestic calendar.

ENTERTAINMENT AND EVENTS
Festivals
PEER GYNT FESTIVAL
(Peer Gynt ved Gålåvatnet)

The annual **Peer Gynt Festival** (www.peergynt.no) is a real highlight on the Norwegian cultural calendar. Taking place on the banks of the Gålåvatnet lake an hour north of Lillehammer, the play brings Henrik Ibsen's dramatic poem to life through song and dance. Although performed in Norwegian, it's subtitled in English through a booklet and audio headset.

In addition to these daily lakeside performances, concerts are held high up in the mountains and in local churches, while art exhibitions and guided hikes around the Gudbrandsdalen valley complete the program. Tickets should be booked well in advance for the 10-day festival, which takes place in early August.

BIRKEBEINERRENNET

The city is the finish line for the world's largest ski race, **Birkebeinerrennet** (www.birkebeiner.no). On a crisp March weekend, more than 12,000 professional and keen amateur skiers complete the epic 54-kilometer (33.5-mile) trail through the mountains east of Lillehammer. Thousands more take part in smaller events over the course of the weekend, including many children.

All participants in the main race carry a backpack weighting 3.5 kilograms (7.7 pounds) to commemorate the original Birkebeinerne that rescued the infant Norwegian prince, Haakon Haakonsson, from a rival faction in 1205-1206. The prince eventually became the king who united Norway after hundreds of years of civil war. The story was immortalized in the 2016 movie *Birkebeinerne,* released internationally as *The Last King.*

FOOD
Cafés and Light Bites
The Italian Renaissance-inspired building of the Kulturhuset Banken theater is the grand setting for **Cafe Stift** (Kirkegata 41, tel. 94 05 31 79, www.cafestift.no, noon-1am Tues.-Fri., noon-3am Sat., 179kr). Despite the imposing exterior, the café itself is light and informal, at least until 9pm, when the food service abruptly stops and the DJs arrive. Up until then, enjoy great-value sandwiches, fish soup, burgers, and even a Norwegian take on a burrito—we won't spoil the surprise—all for well under 200kr.

A heaped plate of miniature Dutch-style pancakes served sweet or salted is the simple yet delicious concept of cottage-like **Det Lille Pannekakehuset** (Storgata 46, tel. 91 99 30 52, 10am-6pm Mon.-Fri., 10am-4pm Sat.), located at the heart of Lillehammer's shopping district. Although savory options and soups are available, one sight of the pancakes covered in berries, ice cream, or chocolate sauce heading out of the kitchen will make up your mind. The sidewalk seating is popular even in the winter, thanks to the blankets and warming cocoa.

New Nordic
The impressive almost-but-not-quite art nouveau exterior of **Hvelvet** (Stortorget 1, tel. 90 72 91 00, www.hvelvet.no, 4pm-11pm Mon.-Sat., 305kr) is hard to miss, and the name (The Vault in Norwegian) hints at the building's history. The former Norges Bank building once held all of Norway's gold reserves, secretly moved from Oslo shortly before the Nazi invasion at the beginning of World War II. The renovated interior is now a fine dining restaurant serving Norwegian ingredients with a touch of Mediterranean flair. The immaculately presented portions are on the small side, so consider the three-course (475kr) or four-course (525kr) set menus, which change monthly.

Chinese
Although less busy than the cluster of restaurants along the main drag of Storgata, **Ming Restaurant** (Storgata 130, tel. 61 26 04 71, 3pm-10pm Tues.-Thurs., 3pm-11pm Fri.-Sat., 2pm-10pm Sun., 189kr) scores highly on all counts. Fragrant dishes from Canton, Beijing, and Sichuan, friendly service, and excellent set menus make this well-kept restaurant the most authentic in the area, despite the simplistic decor.

Pub Food

Riverside sports bar **Nikkers** (Elvegata 18, tel. 61 24 74 30, www.nikkers.no, 11am-11pm Mon.-Thurs., 11am-3am Fri.-Sat., 1pm-10pm Sun.) serves up a British-style pub menu in its separate restaurant. Pick up a lunchtime sandwich or omelet for under 150kr. Most mains run under 200kr, but the house specialty, a fragrant wild game stew and mash, is a great choice for couples at 239kr per person.

Free popcorn sides mean you won't need more than a single course at the stylish **Heim Gastropub** (Storgata 84, tel. 61 10 00 82, www.heim-lillehammer.no, 3pm-noon Mon.-Thurs., 3pm-3pm Fri., noon-3am Sat., 169-229kr). Use that money to instead sample some of the Norwegian brews both bottled and on tap, a staggering range from fresh fruity saison ales through to heavy stouts. The beef bourguignon, battered fish-and-chips, and house burger are better value than the meat and cheese platters, which may still leave you hungry. Despite the late opening hours, the kitchen closes at 10pm.

Although beer is the star of the show at the local brewery's pub, **Lillehammer Bryggeri** (Elvegata 19, tel. 95 01 91 08, www.lillehammerbryggeri.no, 5pm-11pm Wed.-Thurs., 5pm-1am Sat.-Sun., 200kr), you can order plates of filling stew, chicken wings, and cured meats to enjoy alongside the ales in this underground watering hole, tucked away on a back street beside the Mesna river. The small-batch brewery produces an outstanding IPA among its constantly revolving selection. Ask the enthusiastic staff about the best beer pairing for your food and you're likely to make a friend for life.

ACCOMMODATIONS

A former chain hotel now happily independent, ★ **Lillehammer Hotel** (Turisthotellvegen 6, tel. 61 28 60 00, www.lillehammerhotel.no, 1,000kr d) stands above the city, conveniently located between Maihaugen and the Olympic Park. The exterior and hallways of this historic building retain a strong sense of dignified tradition, yet many of its 300 rooms are decked out in a contemporary style with images of winter sports adorning the walls. Two restaurants, two bars, and various lounges mean there are plenty of places to relax after a day on the slopes.

After 130 years as a working millhouse, the tall mustard-colored **Mølla Hotel** (Elvegata 12, tel. 61 05 70 80, www.mollahotell.no, 990kr s, 1,290kr d) is one of Norway's most unique accommodations. Original machinery and thick stone walls leave you in no doubt of the building's history, while Olympic memorabilia on the walls does the same for the city. The cramped rooms are comfortable, but there's little room for spreading out to relax, so most guests head for the hotel's rooftop **Toppen Bar** (8pm-2am Mon.-Sat.) to enjoy an iced cocktail with a view.

The city's best budget option is also one of its best located. Simple, hotel-standard rooms with no-frills hostel-style service are the thing at **Lillehammer Stasjonen Hotel & Hostel** (Jernbanetorget 2, tel. 61 26

00 24, www.stasjonen.no, 850kr s, 950kr d), located inside the railway station. Spacious family rooms (1,400kr) and dorm beds (300kr) are also available. Guests have access to a breakfast buffet (99kr) or lighter options (35kr) in the station café every morning, and a 15 percent discount on lunch and dinner. Check-in after 10pm requires prior arrangement.

Those skiing, visiting Hunderfossen, or just driving through the region should consider the diverse range of hotels, apartments, chalets, and mountain cabins managed by **Hafjell Resort** (tel. 61 28 55 50, www.hafjellresort.no), 16 kilometers (10 miles) north of Lillehammer. A comfortable double room with private bath and buffet breakfast can be booked for 1,090kr.

INFORMATION AND SERVICES

Handily located inside the train station is **Lillehammer Tourist Information** (Jernbanetorget 2, tel. 61 28 98 00, 8am-4pm Mon.-Fri., 10am-2pm Sat.). The staff can help you with accommodation bookings and directions to attractions. Several brochures and city maps are free, although you'll have to pay for the more detailed hiking and skiing maps, which are on sale alongside a small selection of Norwegian souvenirs, postcards, and postage stamps. When the office is closed, brochures about Lillehammer and the surrounding area plus detailed maps are available on the walls outside.

GETTING THERE

The 184-kilometer (114-mile) drive from Oslo to Lillehammer along the E6 highway takes just over two hours, a quicker option than the shorter route using Rv4. Add on an extra 10-15 minutes to reach Hafjell, Hunderfossen Family Park, and the Bob and Luge Track.

NSB (tel. 81 50 08 88, www.nsb.no) runs trains once per hour from Oslo Central Station to Lillehammer, with almost all calling at Oslo Airport on the way. A single ticket bought on the day of the 2.25-hour journey costs 414kr. Four trains per day travel from Trondheim at a cost of 754kr for the 4.5-hour journey. Book your tickets at least 24 hours in advance for a discount of at least 40 percent. **Lillehammer Station** (Jernbanetorget 2) is also home to the city's bus station, a modern waiting room, and a café.

GETTING AROUND

While Lillehammer's compact center is easy to navigate on foot, the steep hills of the surrounding area and harsh winter weather will soon have you looking for other options. The local bus service in and around Lillehammer is managed by **Opplandstrafikk** (Kirkegata 76, tel. 61 28 90 00, www.opplandstrafikk.no). Single tickets within the city cost 37kr, with most travel to/from Hunderfossen/Hafjell covered by a 50kr two-zone ticket. Expect buses to run approximately 7am-10pm, but check timetables for specifics, especially on weekends and late in the evening.

92

For taxi service, call **06565 Drosjene** (tel. 06565, booking@06565.
no), which has cars based in Lillehammer and the Hunderfossen/Hafjell
area. Expect to pay 207-279kr for an eight-kilometer (five-mile) journey,
depending on the time of day. Minimum prices run 102-138kr regardless of distance.

LILLEHAMMER

Background

The Landscape

The development of Norway has been influenced to an extraordinary degree by the mountainous terrain and the historic climate of the region. Although known for its iconic fjords, Norway has some of the most diverse terrain in Europe. From immense glaciers, lush forests, and the highest mountains in northern Europe to the plains of Arctic tundra in the High North and an endless string of skerries, islets, and islands, Norway has natural beauty in abundance.

GEOGRAPHY

Even at more than 2,500 kilometers in length, 70 percent of mainland Norway's landmass is covered with mountains, glaciers, and lakes. Just 4 percent of the land is arable, which is one of the reasons Norway's farming industry is heavily subsidized by the government. The elongated country stretches from 58°N to more than 71°N latitude, with Svalbard lying at 81°N. The north of Norway wraps around the top of the Scandinavian peninsula so much that Kirkenes lies farther east than Finland's capital, Helsinki, and on the same longitude as Saint Petersburg, Russia.

Although Norway's total area is given as 385,199 square kilometers, some 16 percent of that is the Svalbard archipelago, high up in the Arctic Ocean. Mainland Norway's landmass consists mostly of igneous and metamorphic rock. There is very little sedimentary rock, so mining was limited to silver and copper rather than coal.

The striking fjords were created thousands of years ago when the ocean flowed into glacial valleys, cutting deep into the landscape. The after-effects can still be seen today at the innermost arms of the immense Sognefjord, where Norway's longest and deepest fjord almost touches the glaciers that remain.

The 1,700-kilometer-long (1,100-mile-long) Scandinavian Mountains line the center of the country and along the Swedish border to the High North. The geography of these mountains bears a striking similarity to those of Scotland, Ireland, and North America's Appalachian Mountains, leading geologists to believe that it was all one single mountain range prior to the breakup of Pangaea about 175 million years ago.

The mountainous heart of the country means nearly all major towns and cities, including Oslo, Bergen, Trondheim, Stavanger, and Tromsø, hug the coastline or the shoreline of a fjord. On the shores of Lake Mjøsa, Lillehammer is one notable exception, but the surrounding Gudbrandsdalen valley is known for its wealth of flora and fauna and acres of cultivated land. Despite the mountains making much of the country

---

Previous: King's Hand sculpture in Oslo's Kvadraturen district; the Oslo harbor.

uninhabitable, there's plenty of room for everyone, with an astonishing 60,896 kilometers (37,839 miles) of shoreline.

CLIMATE

Heat that the Gulf Stream emits into the atmosphere is vital for the relatively mild climate in Norway. Southern and western coastal areas in particular enjoy warm summers and surprisingly mild, albeit dark and wet, winters. Despite the exposed nature of many Norwegian coastal cities, thousands of small islands off the west coast help to protect the population from the worst of the storms.

Temperature

Were it not for the warming effect of the Gulf Stream, Norway would be up to 25°F colder. To understand this, head away from the coast and over the mountains into the center of the country. Here, where the climate is much less affected by ocean currents, temperatures plummet. The daily mean temperature for February is 2.1°C (35.8°F) in coastal Bergen, 4°C (24.8°F) in Oslo, and -10.4°C (13.3°F) in Røros, far inland. The summers can reach as high as 30°C (86°F) in the major cities, but an average of 20°C (68°F) is more common.

Precipitation

Although the coastal cities are warmer, they must put up with increased rainfall. Bergen and the surrounding fjords are some of the wettest parts of northern Europe. The city receives rainfall an average of 231 days every year, with Stavanger not far behind with 221 days. In contrast, Oslo receives rainfall on only 160 days per year. September through November is the wettest time of the year in almost all the country, while May through July offers the most pleasant weather.

Winters are surprisingly mild, and some coastal areas receive very little snowfall. Broadly speaking, most Norwegian cities can expect snowfall from November through March, with that period extending the farther inland and the farther north you travel.

ENVIRONMENTAL ISSUES
Arctic Drilling

The chief concern among environmentalists in Norway today is the emerging interest in drilling for natural resources in Arctic waters. It is believed that vast quantities of oil and gas reserves lie under the Arctic Ocean, possibly the last major discoveries still to be made on the planet. On the other hand, campaigners view the Arctic as a delicate ecosystem, one of the world's last great wilderness areas and a safe haven for endangered species.

The great irony is that even thinking about drilling is only possible because manmade climate change has caused the Arctic region to warm twice as fast as anywhere else on earth. Melting ice has exposed more of the ocean, making these huge reserves of natural resources more accessible than ever before.

Climate Change

Norwegians are said to be some of the most concerned about climate change, even though its effects will harm Norway significantly less than many other countries. That said, future climate models predict increased precipitation, which risks landslides and floods. As winters become significantly milder, Arctic sea ice may start to disappear, threatening the polar bear on Svalbard and shifting many species northward. Mackerel and red deer have been recorded farther north than ever before.

Despite acid rain decreasing in recent years as a result of reduced emissions across Europe, its effects have damaged lakes, rivers, and forests. In southern Norway, most populations of wild salmon have disappeared.

Melting Glaciers

Norway's glaciers continue to recede at an alarming rate. Since 1986, the total area covered by glaciers has decreased by 11 percent, and the most pessimistic predictions claim some of Norway's glaciers could disappear completely by 2030. The effect is more marked in the Svalbard archipelago, where glaciers are on average losing 23-27 inches of their thickness every single year.

History

EARLY HISTORY

The land now known as Norway emerged from the Ice Age thanks to the warming effect of the Gulf Stream. The glacial land became habitable from around 12,000 BC, with good conditions for sealing, fishing, and hunting along the coastline attracting immigration. Although it is believed people arrived earlier, the oldest human skeleton found in Norway was carbon dated to 6,600 BC. It was found in the waters of the Sognefjord as recently as 1994.

As people in the north began to travel on basic wooden skis and use slate tools, the Oslofjord region became suitable for farming thanks to technology from farther south. Sometime around 2,500 BC, farming spread quickly northward across the country, with oats, barley, pigs, cattle, sheep, and goats becoming commonplace.

Fertile areas around the Oslofjord, Trondheimsfjord, Lake Mjøsa (near Lillehammer), and Jæren (near Stavanger) began to create wealth for farming communities. Around the advent of the Common Era, speakers of Uralic languages arrived in the north and mixed with the indigenous population, becoming the Sami people.

The Iron Age allowed for easier cultivation, and thus new areas were cleared as the population grew with the increased harvests. A new social

Inside a Viking Home

The ships found in the Viking burial mounds along the Oslofjord are spectacular, but it's what's inside them that has given us a far greater understanding of what daily life was like.

The Viking apron-dress was worn suspended over the shoulders by paired brooches hooked through narrow looped straps, and worn over a smock or gown. Fewer finds of clothing exist for Viking men than for Viking women because men tended to be cremated, but it seems that the basics of men's clothing in Scandinavia changed little throughout the Viking Age. Materials of trousers, tunics, coats, and cloaks changed from leather to wool to linen, but style changed little. Many textiles were made of carefully woven wool, attractively textured and often dyed in bright colors.

The Vikings ate two meals each day. The first was eaten in the morning, around two hours after the day's work was started (around 8am), while the second was consumed at the end of the day's work, around 7pm. Exact times would vary seasonally. Beef, mutton, lamb, goat, pork, and horsemeat were eaten, along with fish and whale. Root vegetables, plus plentiful plums, apples, and blackberries were common accompaniments.

While alcoholic beverages (most notably ale and mead) played an important role in festivities, the Vikings had an acute awareness of the perils and dangers of drunkenness.

structure evolved: When sons married, they would remain in the same house; such an extended family was a clan. They would offer protection from other clans; if conflicts arose, the issue would be decided at a *thing*, a sacred place where all freemen from the surrounding area would assemble and could determine punishments for crimes, such as paying fines in food. The word *thing* is still used today to refer to council chambers. The Norwegian Parliament, Stortinget, literally translates as "The Big Thing."

From the first century AD a cultural influence from the Roman Empire took place. Norwegians created a runic alphabet and began trading furs and skins for luxury items. Some of the most powerful farmers became chieftains, and their power increased during the Migration Period between 400 and 550, as other Germanic tribes migrated northward and local farmers wanted protection.

VIKING ERA

Perhaps the most famous period in Norwegian history, the Viking Age was a period of expansion not just for Norway, but for the whole Nordic region. Far from just barbaric, axe-wielding invaders, the Vikings created complex social institutions, oversaw the coming of Christianity to Scandinavia, and left a major impact on European history through trade, colonization, and far-flung exploration.

The first record of the Vikings was the late 8th-cenutry invasion of Lindisfarne, an island off the northeast coast of England. It was quite the way to announce themselves, as at the time, Lindisfarne monastery was considered one of the great sanctuaries of the Christian church in western Europe.

The *Anglo-Saxon Chronicle* stated: "In this year fierce, foreboding omens came over the land of the Northumbrians, and the wretched people shook; there were excessive whirlwinds, lightning, and fiery dragons were seen flying in the sky. These signs were followed by great famine, and a little after those, that same year on 6th ides of January, the ravaging of wretched heathen people destroyed God's church at Lindisfarne."

Vikings proceeded to raid a monastery at Jarrow in Northumbria. with southern Wales and Ireland falling victim to invasions soon after. Over a thousand Old Norse words influenced modern English, along with more than 1,000 place-names in northeastern England and the Scottish islands. Vikings were well trained, with good weapons and chain-mail armor, and their belief that being killed in battle resulted in them going to Valhalla gave them a psychological advantage in battle for many years.

Misconceptions about the Vikings remain today. For example, the myth that Vikings wore horned helmets was actually an invention of 19th-century Romanticism. Although many women stayed to look after the household during Viking raids, some women and even children traveled with the men. One of the most fearsome Viking commanders was a woman, known as the Red Maiden.

The raids produced riches and slaves, which the Vikings brought back to Scandinavia to work the farms. As farmland grew scarce and resistance against the invasions grew in England, the Vikings began to look at targets further afield, such as Iceland, Greenland, and Newfoundland.

During the 9th century, the largest chieftains began a long period of civil war, until King Harald Fairhair was able to unite the country and create the first Norwegian state.

Early Vikings saw Christianity as a heretical threat to their own pagan beliefs. Christian monks and missionaries were active in Scandinavia throughout the Viking Age, but it took until the era of Olav Tryggvason (963-1000) for the tide to begin to change. He is believed to have built Norway's first church, although information about him is sparse. He did, however, found the city of Trondheim (then called Nidaros), and a statue of him today stands high above the city's main square.

Following Tryggvason's death, it was Olav Haraldsson who began to pass church laws, destroyed pagan temples, build churches, and appoint priests. As many chieftains feared that Christianization would rob them of power, it took centuries for Christianity to be fully accepted. For years many people adopted both religions as an insurance policy in case one didn't work out. Evidence of this can be seen today in the carvings on some of Norway's oldest stave churches, which feature figures from Norse mythology.

After almost a century of peace, civil war broke out in 1130 because on ambiguous rules of succession. The newly-created Archdiocese of Nidaros attempted to control the appointment of kings, which led to the church taking sides in the various battles. In 1217, Håkon Håkonsson introduced a clear law of succession.

Through the 11th and 12th centuries, population increased drastically and farms began to be subdivided, with many landowners turning over parts of their land to the king or the church in challenging times. Throughout the 13th century a tithe of around twenty percent of a farmer's yield went to the landowners.

Norway's Golden Age—at least until the much more recent discovery of oil—is widely accepted to be the late 13th and early 14th centuries. It was a time of peace and growing international trade with Britain and Germany, most notably the Hanseatic League (a commercial federation of merchant guilds founded in Germany that dominated northern European trade for centuries), which took control of trade through Bergen. However, this time of prosperity came to an abrupt end in 1349 as the Black Death arrived in Norway and killed a third of the population within a year. Many communities were entirely wiped out and the subsequent reduction in tax income weakened the king's position and the church became increasingly powerful.

BACKGROUND
HISTORY

POLITICAL UNIONS

In 1380 Olav Haakonsson inherited the thrones of both Norway and Denmark and created a union, the start of a long period of political alliances and wars between the Scandinavian countries. Seventeen years later, the Kalmar Union was created between Norway, Denmark, and Sweden. Although the ruling Margaret I pursued a centralizing policy that favored Denmark's greater population, Norway was too weak economically to pull out of the union. Supported by Margaret, the Hanseatic League formed its own state within the city of Bergen, further weakening Norway's status.

Norway continued to play a minor role in the union until Sweden declared independence in the 1520s. This created a Denmark-Norway nation ruled from Copenhagen. Frederick I of Denmark favored Martin Luther's Reformation and initially agreed not to introduce Protestantism to Norway, but in 1529 he proceeded to begin the process.

The Catholic resistance within Norway was led by Olav Engelbrektsson but found little support. Christian III formally introduced Lutheranism, demoted Norway to the status of a Danish province, and introduced the Danish written language, although Norwegian dialects remained in place. During the 17th century, Denmark entered into a series of territorial wars with Sweden, which culminated in the Great Northern War (1700-1721) in which a Russian-led coalition ended the supremacy of the Swedish empire in northern Europe. Toward the end of the war, Swedish forces tried unsuccessfully to invade Trondheim. Norway's economy grew thanks in part to the timber trade, and the population grew from around 150,000 in

1500 to around 900,000 in 1800. Many Norwegians earned a living as sailors in foreign ships, especially the Dutch ships that came for the timber.

To avoid deforestation, a royal decree closed a large number of sawmills in 1688; because this mostly affected farmers with small mills, by the mid-18th century only a handful of merchants controlled the entire lumber industry. Mining, including the Kongsberg silver mines and Røros copper mines; shipping; and fishing became the chief drivers of the economy.

Throughout the period, Bergen was the largest town in the country, twice the size of Christiania (now Oslo) and Trondheim combined.

AN INDEPENDENT NATION

The economy suffered as Denmark-Norway backed France in the Napoleonic Wars, and soon Sweden took an interest in Norway. Following defeat at the Battle of Leipzig in 1813, the Crown Prince of Denmark-Norway and resident viceroy in Norway, Christian Frederik, began a Norwegian independence movement. A national assembly was called at Eidsvoll, but rather than elect Frederik as an absolute monarch the 112 members instead chose to form a constitution. It was written over the course of five weeks and adopted on May 17, 1814, the date celebrated today as Norwegian Constitution Day. The constitution split the nation's power between a king, a position to which Christian Frederik was appointed, and a new parliamentary body.

Just weeks after the signing of the constitution, King Carl Johan of Sweden invaded Norway, and due to economic troubles, Norway accepted Swedish rule, albeit with their constitution intact. Rather than an independence day, May 17 became an important political rally every year. In search of a better life, Norwegians began leaving rural Norway for North America in 1825, with mass emigration occurring over the following 100 years. By 1930, approximately 800,000 people had left Norway, with the majority settling in the American Midwest, where Norwegian heritage and traditions remain strong to this day.

Improvements in agricultural technology and transport infrastructure, notably a railroad that connected Oslo with Trondheim for the first time, helped to grow the economy during the late 19th century. The shipping industry enjoyed a boom, and by 1880 there were 60,000 Norwegian seamen. In 1913, Norway became the second country in Europe after Finland to give women the vote, after years of campaigning from liberal politician Gina Krog.

Although Norway adopted a policy of neutrality from 1905, the Norwegian merchant marine supported the British in World War I. Half the fleet was sunk and thousands of seamen were killed. The interwar period was dominated by economic instability, caused among other things by a succession of short-term governments, strikes, lockouts, and deflation.

Forces of Nazi Germany occupied Norway from the beginning to the end of World War II. The German goal was to use Norway to control access to the North Sea and the Atlantic, and to station air and naval forces to prevent convoys traveling between Britain and the USSR.

The government in exile, including the royal family, escaped to London. Politics were suspended and the government coordinated action with the Allies, retained control of a world-wide diplomatic and consular service, and operated the huge Norwegian merchant marine. It organized and supervised the resistance within Norway, which numbered 40,000 by the end of the war. The home front relied on sabotage, raids, clandestine operations, and intelligence gathering to hinder German operations. One of the most successful actions undertaken by the Norwegian resistance was the heavy water sabotage, which crippled the German nuclear energy project and has since been immortalized in several books and TV series.

The economic consequences of the German occupation were severe. Trading partners were lost, and although Germany stepped in, it could not totally replace the lost export business, and in fact confiscated more than half of what was produced within Norway. Because of this, and combined with a drop in productivity, Norwegians were quickly confronted with scarcity of food, so many turned to growing their own crops and keeping livestock.

In the latter years of the war, Hitler's scorched earth policy left a lasting impact on Finnmark. Transport infrastructure and homes were burned to the ground, with populations fleeing to the mountains and living in caves. In early 1945, returning Norwegian forces slowly took back the region and helped the remaining population to deal with the harsh Arctic winter and occasional German air raids.

POST-WAR RECOVERY

The immediate post-war years saw an increase in Nordic collaboration, including the creation of Scandinavian Airlines System (SAS) and the Nordic Council. Norway started negotiations for the creation of a Scandinavian defense union, but instead opted to become a founding member of the North Atlantic Treaty Organization (NATO). The Labour Party retained power throughout this period and enforced a policy of public planning. Construction of new railroads, hydroelectricity plants, aluminum works, and a steel mill helped the country to recover, as did the hosting of the 1952 Winter Olympics in Oslo.

Throughout the post-war period, fishing and agriculture became more mechanized, while agricultural subsidies rose to the third highest in the world. Heavy industry grew in the 1960s, and Norway became Europe's largest exporter of aluminum.

THE OIL ERA

In 1969, oil was discovered in the Ekofisk field, which would eventually become one of the largest oil fields in the world. The emerging industry not only created jobs in production, but a large number of supply and technology companies were established. High petroleum taxes and dividends from state-run Statoil earned the government significant reventues.

Stavanger in particular experienced a boom as an international workforce descended on the city, but the oil boom wasn't all great news. In 1977, Ekofisk experienced a major blowout, and 123 people were killed when the Alexander Kielland accommodation rig capsized in 1980. Regulation increased, and by 1990 Norway was Europe's largest oil producer.

The population rejected EU membership in a 1994 referendum, but the country joined the European Economic Area and the Schengen Area (an area comprising 26 European states that have officially abolished passport and border control at their mutual borders). These decisions contributed to the rise in population from 4.2 million in 1990 to 5.2 million in 2016. Population growth is expected to continue and hit 6 million sometime before 2030.

Government and Economy

POLITICS

Norway is a constitutional monarchy, currently led by King Harald V. In practice the king has very little political power, as all legislative power resides in the elected Parliament led by a prime minister. Despite this, Norway's royal family remains popular throughout the country.

Norway's multi-party system tends to result in coalition governments, although the Labour Party (Arbeiderpartiet) has traditionally seen the most success. Since World War II, Labour Party governments have often relied on the support of other socialist and left-leaning parties to form a government.

However, in 2013 the Conservative (Høyre) leader Erna Solberg was able to form a center-right coalition with the Progress Party (Fremskrittspartiet), even though the Labour Party won 30.8 percent of the popular vote and won the most seats. Currently, eight parties are represented within the Norwegian Parliament.

Generally speaking, Norwegians trust in their political process and therefore turnout at both general and local elections is relatively high.

ECONOMY

Norway consistently tops the standard of living when compared with other European countries, helped by a strong welfare system. The system, along with the country's agricultural and manufacturing systems, relies heavily on a "savings account" created from the oil and gas wealth. The value of the Government Pension Fund of Norway (commonly referred to as the Oil Fund) constantly fluctuates but fund manager Norges Bank maintains a running total on its website (www.norges-bank.no).

The country's workforce is heavily unionized, and most employees, both public and private, are a member of at least one trade body.

Central, regional, and local governments are major employers throughout Norway. Many government departments are located around the country to help with job creation, such as the register of businesses at Brønnøysund, midway between Trondheim and Bodø.

Petroleum and natural gas remain Norway's most important private sector industries. Seafood is a thriving export business, including smoked salmon from the country's turbulent rivers and dried fish products from Lofoten.

Future Economy

Because of the oil boom since the 1970s, there has been little government incentive to help develop and encourage new industries in the private sector, in contrast to other Nordic countries like Sweden and particularly Finland. However, the government has committed significant cash to the Innovation Norway organization, which is charged with stimulating the future Norwegian economy by helping companies to develop their competitive advantage and enhance innovation.

While the country's tech startup community lags behind Nordic neighbors Sweden and Finland, new business ventures are finding success in the research, development, and commercialization of new processes and technologies for the energy, seafood, and maritime industries.

People and Culture

DEMOGRAPHY AND DIVERSITY

Citizens of Norway are primarily ethnic Norwegians of north Germanic descent. Outside of Norway, the largest concentration of the ethnic group exists in the United States, where an estimated four million ethnic Norwegians live as a result of the mass migration 100-150 years ago. Canada and Brazil also have large numbers of ethnic Norwegians among their populations.

Other than recent economic migrants, the main demographic diversity is provided by the indigenous Sami people, who settled across the north of Scandinavia around 8,000 years ago.

The Sami People

The Sami are an indigenous people known as nomadic reindeer herders, although only a few thousand still participate. The rest make their living through fishing, farming, and hunting, and a great many have moved elsewhere in Norway to work in the modern service sector.

Sami people are known for their colorful knitted dress and the *joik*, a form of song dedicated to a person, animal, or place. Each Sami has their own melody, and traditionally a young Sami boy will compose a unique *yoik* for the girl he is courting. Many traditional melodies are still alive, having been handed down for generations. The lavish outfits resplendent with jewelry used to be in daily use, whereas today the outfits are reserved for special occasions, or to welcome tourists.

Many varieties of the Sami language, a Uralic language with no connection to Norwegian, are under threat as the number of native speakers continues to drop. To help combat this, national broadcaster NRK runs a Sami-only radio station, while schoolchildren can now choose to continue their studies on to higher education in their native language.

Based upon the Norwegian constitution and the Sami Act of 1987, the Sami are recognized indigenous people of Norway and as such are entitled to special protections and rights. In particular, a national Sami Parliament of 37 elected representatives works with political issues relevant to Sami people and has responsibility for a budget of more than 400 million kroner. Much of the land in Finnmark, Norway's vast northeastern county, is managed by the Parliament.

Before the Sami Parliament was initiated, a political movement began when power company Statkraft planned to dam the Alta River in Finnmark. The case known as the Alta Controversy united the environmental and Sami interest groups, and although the dam was eventually built, the political fallout led to the end of the controversial "Norwegianization" policy of the government and the eventual creation of the Sami Parliament.

RELIGION

The Church of Norway has dominated religion in Norway for around 1,000 years. It has belonged to the Evangelical Lutheran branch of the Christian church since the 16th century, and was until very recently the official church of the Norwegian state.

The separation of the Church of Norway from the Norwegian state began in 2008 and is still ongoing. As a result of the initial changes, Norway now has no formal state religion, the government will not participate in the appointment of church deans and bishops, and there is no longer a requirement that at least half of the government ministers must belong to the Lutheran Church. As of 2017, the Church of Norway is an entirely separate entity from the state.

It is important to note that the constitution still establishes the Church of Norway as "The People's Church" and establishes Norway's values as stemming from "our Christian and Humanist heritage." The constitution also still requires monarchs to swear allegiance to "God the all-knowing and almighty" when they are sworn into office, and they are still obliged to adhere to the Evangelical Lutheran faith of the Church of Norway.

The separation of church and state reflects a broader rise in atheism across Norway. In 2016, a national survey revealed that more Norwegians don't believe in God than do, for the first time.

LANGUAGE

Norwegian is a Scandinavian language, a collection of North Germanic languages closely related to one another. Native speakers of Norwegian, Swedish, and Danish can to a large extent understand one another even though the languages are distinct. Faroese and Icelandic, whilst also being North Germanic, because of their differences are not considered Scandinavian languages.

The heritage of all the North Germanic languages lies in the Old Norse language spoken by the Vikings. Originally the people of what is now Norway spoke a Western Old Norse dialect, which developed into the Icelandic and Faroese of today. A long period of political union with Denmark resulted in Danish being introduced across Norway, eventually splintering to become a distinct language.

Because of this history, there are actually two forms of written Norwegian, Bokmål and Nynorsk. Bokmål (book language) is the dominant form, taught as standard in 86.5 percent of schools, and is the language of urban Norway. Nynorsk (new Norwegian) was created as an alternative to the Danish-influenced Bokmål in the 19th century. It is used mainly in rural municipalities of western Norway, where you may find spellings of place-names and attractions that differ slightly from those listed in this guide.

Strong dialects are commonplace and more or less fall into four regional variants: North, West, South, and East, but dialects exist right down to a local level. Politicians and TV presenters often use their local dialects, which can make learning and understanding Norwegian more problematic.

In parts of northern Norway, Sami languages are spoken and appear on road signs alongside Norwegian. In Kirkenes, you'll even see road signs in Norwegian and Russian.

Norwegians are some of the best nonnative speakers of English in the world. Norwegian children learn English from the first year of school. In addition, British and American television is commonplace and almost always subtitled rather than dubbed. Some of the older generation may struggle with speaking English, but 99 percent of Norwegians you meet will understand every word you say.

LITERATURE

Other than original pagan Eddaic poetry from the Viking era, the first significant Norwegian literature came as a result of the learnings from the introduction of Christianity. *Historia Norwegiæ* is a short history of Norway written in Latin by an anonymous monk, while the speculum piece *Konungs skuggsjá (King's Mirror)* deals with politics and morality.

The next significant period of Norwegian literature wasn't until the struggle for independence from Denmark. The dramatist Henrik Wergeland was the most influential author of the period, while the works of Henrik Ibsen were consumed around the world. His fairy-tale-inspired five-act play *Peer Gynt* is still performed today.

Crime is the number one fiction genre across Scandinavia today and is characterized by its plain, direct writing style that's high on descriptive setting and low on metaphor. It is especially popular around Easter, when many television channels run detective shows and crime movie marathons. Jo Nesbø, Jørn Lier Horst, and the former Minister of Justice Anne Holt are some of the leading names to look out for.

VISUAL ARTS
Artists

Norwegian art came into its own in the 19th century as the influence of Danish rule began to erode and a new sense of identity gripped the nation. Landscape painting from the era remains one of the best examples of Norwegian art and dominates many of the country's galleries. Johan Christian Dahl (1788-1857) is often said to be the "father of Norwegian landscape painting." His notable works include *Vinter ved Sognefjorden (Winter by the Sognefjord)* and *Skibbrudd ved den norske kyst (Shipwreck on the Norwegian coast),* both of which are in the collection of Oslo's National Gallery.

Many keen young painters studied in France and brought back Impressionism and Realism, which gradually became more popular within Norway.

The intense psychological themes in the works of Edvard Munch (1863-1944) are arguably Norway's most famous cultural export. His 1893 painting *The Scream* features a figure with an agonized expression on a bridge with a fiery sky in the backdrop. Four versions of the work exist, which have been targets for numerous theft attempts and the subject of many parodies.

Nikolai Astrup (1880-1928) spent time in France and Germany before returning to Jølster in western Norway, where he became one of the greatest Norwegian artists from the early 20th century. Only recently becoming known outside of Norway, his neo-romantic landscapes are known for their vivid colors.

Film

The dramatic scenery of Norway has become a popular location for TV and movie makers, and the government now offers tax incentives to tempt international studios.

Battle scenes on the ice planet Hoth from the Star Wars movie *The Empire Strikes Back* were filmed around the tiny village of Finse, high up in the mountains between Oslo and Bergen, while parts of Svalbard and Jostedalsbreen National Park were used to film scenes for the James Bond movie *Die Another Day.* Large parts of the science-fiction psychological thriller *Ex Machina* were shot on location at the Juvet Landscape Hotel in Valldalen.

In recent years the Norwegian movie industry has produced some notable works of its own. The horror movie *Død Snø (Dead Snow)*, dark fantasy mockumentary *Trollhunter*, and disaster movie *Bølgen (The Wave)* have all found a cult following outside of Norway.

MUSIC

Composers Edvard Grieg (1843-1907) and Johan Svendsen (1840-1911) were leading composers of the Romantic era and played a pivotal role in forming Norwegian national identity following the end of Danish rule. Both composers added elements of Norwegian folk music to European classical traditions to create a distinctive Norwegian sound.

Many traditional styles of folk music have died out, aside from the traditional Sami *joik*, which has enjoyed something of a revival in recent years. Having said that, Norwegian folk music does still influence the contemporary music of today. The progressive rock band Gåte rearranged traditional folk tunes and performed in a heavy central Norwegian dialect.

The country enjoys a strong choir tradition, especially in smaller rural towns. This tradition can be traced back to the 12th century, with a resurgence during the 19th century around the time of independence.

Contemporary styles from jazz to rap are popular, but artists with international success are limited. Norway is, however, noted for its electronic and dance music scene, with artists like Röyksopp and Bel Canto becoming worldwide names. In the 1980s, Norwegian pop group A-ha achieved meteoric international success when the trio's 1985 debut *Take On Me* shot to number one in the United States and the United Kingdom. The band, led by vocalist Morten Harket, went on to sell more than 80 million records worldwide.

Essentials

Transportation

GETTING THERE
Air

Almost all international visitors to Norway will arrive at the modern **Oslo Airport Gardermoen** (OSL), which is also the main domestic hub for connections to all parts of the country.

FROM NORTH AMERICA

Scandinavian Airlines (SAS) (www.flysas.com) operates nonstop flights to Oslo from Newark and Miami. SAS also operates services to Stockholm and Copenhagen from Chicago, San Francisco, Los Angeles, and Washington-Dulles. A connecting flight to Oslo is usually included at no extra or little additional cost.

At the time of writing, low-cost airline **Norwegian** (www.norwegian.com) flies to Oslo from Boston, Fort Lauderdale, Las Vegas, Los Angeles, New York JFK, Oakland, and Orlando. The schedules vary seasonally, and due to the limited number of weekly departures (usually one or two per route), delays can have severe knock-on effects across the network.

SAS's Star Alliance partner **United** (www.united.com) offers an additional service between Newark and Oslo, while KLM, Air France, British Airways, Lufthansa, and Icelandair offer connections from many North American airports via Amsterdam, Paris, London, Frankfurt, and Reykjavik, respectively. **Icelandair** (www.icelandair.com) in particular is a popular option because it allows free stopovers to add a night in Reykjavik to your itinerary.

FROM EUROPE

Both SAS and Norwegian offer a vast network of flights to Oslo from European destinations, with connections to the United Kingdom and Spain particularly strong. Along with the major flag-carriers such as British Airways, Lufthansa, and KLM, low-cost airline **Ryanair** (www.ryanair.com) currently flies to Oslo from destinations including London Stansted and Manchester, but the latter along with eight other routes land at Sandefjord Airport Torp, one of the few Norwegian airports not operated by state-run Avinor. Despite the budget airline listing the airport as Oslo, it is almost two hours by bus from the city.

SAS tends to run flights to its hubs in Copenhagen and Stockholm, while Norwegian runs flights to London Gatwick and many vacation spots in the Mediterranean.

Previous: fish, a Norwegian staple; Oslofjord with the city of Oslo in the background.

Car or Motorcycle

Many travelers from northern Europe enter Norway in their own car or a rented vehicle to avoid the relatively high cost of rental within Norway. As Norway and Sweden are both Schengen countries, the multiple border crossings are always open, but occasional customs checks do take place. The busiest border crossing is the Svinesundsbrua bridge on the E6 highway between Oslo and Gotheburg.

Driving licenses issued in the EU/EEA are valid for driving in Norway as long as they are valid in the country they were issued. Driving licenses issued outside the EU/EEA are valid for driving in Norway for up to three months.

Bus

Long-distance coach services are available from across northern Europe and are often the cheapest method of transportation. **Oslo Bus Terminal** (Schweigaards gate 6-14) is the arrival point for all international bus routes. **Swebus** (www.swebus.se) runs regular coaches from Stockholm, Gothenburg, and Copenhagen, from where **Eurolines** (tel. +49/6196 2078 501, www.eurolines.de) offers connections from Berlin, Frankfurt, and Hamburg. **Czech Transport** (tel. +420/776 677 890 Mon.-Fri., www.czech-transport.com) runs a weekly service from Prague.

Rail

Oslo Central Station (Jernbanetorget 1, tel. 81 50 08 88, www.oslo-s.no) is linked into the European rail network via Swedish cities Gothenburg and Stockholm. Three daily trains make the four-hour journey from Gothenburg, and tickets can be booked via the Norwegian state railway company **NSB** (tel. 81 50 08 88, www.nsb.no), but to make the five-hour journey from Stockholm, you must book in advance with the Swedish state company **SJ** (tel. +46/771 757575, www.sj.se).

If you are arriving by rail and plan to continue your journey around Norway by rail, it's worth investigating the European rail passes on offer. Non-Europeans can use **Eurail** (www.eurail.com) and European citizens **Interrail** (interrail.eu). Both passes are especially good value for those under 25 and for families traveling together.

Boat

In addition to the increasing numbers of cruise ships, three international ferry operators service Oslo. **DFDS** (tel. +44/330 333 0245, www.dfdssea-ways.co.uk) operates overnight boats from Copenhagen, while **Color Line** (tel. 81 00 08 11, www.colorline.no) runs a daily service to and from Kiel in northern Germany. Finally, **Stena Line** (tel. 23 17 91 30, www.stenaline.no) operates a 24-hour return service to and from Fredrikshavn in northern Denmark, known locally as a "booze cruise"; Oslo locals take advantage of the duty-free regulations on board, often stumbling back into Oslo with crates of beer in tow.

Bus

Long-distance buses are usually the cheapest but slowest option for moving between Norway's cities. Budget-concious travelers should book in advance with **Lavprisekspressen** (www.lavprisekspressen.no) for cheap deals.

For a wider network of destinations across south and central Norway, **NOR-WAY Bussekspress** (tel. 81 54 44 44, www.nor-way.no) runs a network of well-established routes.

Car

Driving in Norway outside the cities is a relatively pleasurable experience. Roads can be quiet and speed limits are low, so taking your time is strongly recommended given the spectacular scenery on offer. Journeys between towns should be carefully planned to take into account potential ferry crossings. These can add substantial time and cost to your journey.

THE ROAD SYSTEM

Any road designated E (e.g., E6, E18) is part of the European highway system and tends to be better maintained. They are double-lane in the vicinity of cities but can be single-lane in rural areas.

The rest of the road system is split between national roads (Rv) and county roads (Fv). The designation refers to which authority has responsibility for maintenance and is of little relevance to travelers. In fact, most road signs and maps will just reference the route number without the Fv/Rv designation.

ROAD CONDITIONS

Road conditions are generally good, but snow and high winds can cause even major highways to close temporarily during the winter months. It's worth checking with the **Norwegian Public Roads Administration (Statens vegvesen)** (tel. 91 50 20 30, www.vegvesen.no) if you are planning any road trip outside the summer season.

RULES OF THE ROAD

On motorways and some highways, speed limits are 90kph or 100kph. On all other roads outside built-up areas, the limit is 80kph unless otherwise indicated. In built-up areas the speed limit is 50kph unless indicated, but can drop as low as 30kph.

It is compulsory for all drivers of all vehicles, including RVs, cars, motorcycles, and mopeds, to have their headlights on at all times. Headlamp beam deflectors may be required. Warning triangles and reflective jackets are compulsory accessories for all private vehicles, so be sure to check your rental car is properly equipped. Hefty on-the-spot fines can be issued for failing to carry specific items. Drivers and passengers of motorcycles and mopeds must wear a crash helmet, while a vehicle towing a caravan must be equipped with special rearview mirrors.

Car rental is expensive by international standards, with daily rates from most known brands starting from 500kr. Advance booking is wise in the summer and essential if you are planning on driving away from smaller airports, as many rental desks only open based on reservations.

Small cars with engines under 2.0L offer the best value and will easily be enough for a couple with luggage. Both gasoline (petrol) and diesel cars are commonplace. Gasoline prices vary but are typically 11-14kr per liter. Diesel tends to be about 10 percent higher. Prices will be higher for all fuel outside of cities and in the north of the country. Many rental companies offer hybrid cars that will save considerable gasoline costs, especially if you are driving around mountainous terrain. The market for electric cars continues to boom in Norway and they are available from most rental companies. Although the charging infrastructure is generally good across the country, it may be best to ask for a gasoline/diesel model if you are unfamiliar with how the charging process works or if you are planning long road trips.

Your rental company will provide breakdown cover. Alternatively, contact the **Norwegian Automobile Association (Norges Automobil-Forbund)** (tel. 92 60 85 05, naf.no), known as NAF, for advice.

Visas and Officialdom

PASSPORTS AND TOURIST VISAS

Immigration paperwork is straightforward for the vast majority of international arrivals who are visiting Norway for tourism. As Norway is a member of the European Schengen Agreement, passport checks are not required for international arrivals from the 25 other members of the Schengen Area. Two notable omissions from the Schengen Area are the United Kingdom and Ireland. This means that if you arrive in Oslo from a connection in Amsterdam, for example, then you will clear immigration into the Schengen Area in Amsterdam, not in Oslo.

Citizens of the United Kingdom and Ireland are free to visit Norway without the need for a visa, as are citizens of the United States, Canada, Mexico, Australia, New Zealand, and many other non-European Union (EU)/European Economic Area (EEA) countries. People who fall into this category are free to stay in Norway (and indeed, the whole Schengen Area) for up to 90 days.

CUSTOMS

Although a member of the Schengen Agreement, Norway's status outside the European Union means it sets its own customs rules. Tourists can bring an unlimited amount of luggage, including clothing, electronics, and jewelry, for use during their stay that they take with them when they leave.

It is forbidden to import any meat and dairy products from outside the EEA. Cash above 25,000kr (or the foreign currency equivalent) must be declared to the Customs Office on arrival.

Tobacco and Alcohol

Alcohol and tobacco quotas are strictly enforced. The amount of alcohol you can bring into the country (which includes purchases at the duty-free stores on arrival) depends on whether you bring tobacco or not. With up to 200 cigarettes or 250 grams of tobacco, you are entitled to bring one liter of spirits, 1.5 liters of wine, and 2 liters of beer. If you forgo the liter of spirits, the quota for beer or wine can increase. Without cigarettes or tobacco, you are permitted to bring 1 liter of spirits, 3 liters of wine, and 2 liters of beer. Again, forgoing the spirit allowance increases the allowance for wine or beer.

You must be at least 18 to bring beer, wine, and tobacco products to Norway, and at least 20 to bring beverages over 22 percent alcohol content. Detailed information on the exact quotas is available from **Norwegian Customs (Toll)** (tel. 22 86 03 12, www.toll.no).

POLICE

Uniformed officers and white squad cars of the **Norwegian Police (Politi)** (www.politi.no) are a regular sight around Norwegian cities. As a general rule, officers are more than happy to give directions to tourists. The emergency number for the police is 112, or 02800 to be put through to the nearest regional police district.

Norwegian police officers are in general respected by the population. In the unlikely event you feel the need to file a complaint, contact the relevant regional police district, where the police chief will consider the complaint within one month. If you disagree with the decision, there is an appeal process overseen by the National Police Directorate.

Food

Abundant fish and seafood, succulent lamb and reindeer, and sharp mountain berries are among the highlights of the Norwegian kitchen. The trend of New Nordic cooking, which combines local seasonal ingredients with an international flair, is rapidly replacing traditional Norwegian dishes from a time when meat and fish had to be preserved by salting and drying.

The same international influence dominates the lower end. You're more likely to find pasta, pizza, hamburgers, and the Norwegian take on a taco rather than traditional favorites such as meatballs or cod. In many restaurants, the menu bears a striking resemblance to what you would find in any western country.

Because of the high cost of wages, prices are high for food across the board. This means that high-end restaurants often represent better value than their cheaper counterparts.

MEALTIMES

Be prepared to adjust your mealtimes. A typical Norwegian lunch is eaten between 11am and 1pm and often consists of bread topped with ham, salami, or cheese. Dinner is taken between 4pm and 7pm and traditionally consists of meat or fish with boiled potatoes and a vegetable, although nowadays pizza is the number one choice in the family home. Restaurants follow these times, and you may struggle to find a kitchen taking orders after 10pm.

The typical Scandinavian breakfast buffet features freshly baked breads with a selection of hams, cheeses, and other cold cuts along with lashings of coffee. The higher-end hotels will offer hot options and fresh juices.

MEAT

Roasted meats are commonplace, although beef tends to be roughly ground with onion and formed into meatcakes *(kjøttkaker)* or meatballs *(kjøttboller)*, typically served with potatoes and a thick brown sauce.

Lamb and mutton are popular around Easter and in the fall. Popular dishes include the national dish, *fårikål* (mutton and cabbage stew), and the traditional Christmas dish *pinnekjøtt* (slow-cooked cured mutton ribs).

Pork roast and chops are popular, as is reindeer, which tends to be served as a steak or in cured sausage form. Reindeer has a distinct, strong taste and is often served with crushed juniper berries and a sour lingonberry jam.

Whale *(hval)* meat is available from high-end restaurants in most parts of Norway. As a traditional food, its consumption is considered less controversial than in many other parts of the world. The lean meat is surprisingly tender and tastes more like beef than anything from the sea.

FISH AND SEAFOOD

After oil, fish and seafood remain Norway's most important exports, and with good reason. The outstanding Norwegian smoked salmon is eaten all around the world, while the fresh variety is a staple feature on Norwegian menus.

Cod is still caught in large numbers along the Norwegian coast, although the most popular variety comes from around the Lofoten islands. Traditionally poached and served with a simple accompaniment of boiled potatoes and carrots, cod is also dried (either by air or salt) and shipped out around the world in vast numbers. The most famous preparation of preserved fish is the traditional Christmas dish lutefisk. Originally prepared before the days of refrigeration, lutefisk is dried cod that is steeped in lye. The gelatinous dish is popular amongst the older generation and at Christmastime but is rarely eaten by the general population.

Fish soup is popular throughout the country and is often one of the cheapest options on a restaurant menu. Recipes vary regionally, but typically the milk-based soup includes 2-3 types of fish with carrots, onions, and potato.

Shrimp is a popular fast food and is prepared simply with a dash of lemon juice, served with bread and butter. Recent decades have seen an explosion of king crabs along the Arctic coast of Norway, increasing the availability of crab legs in Arctic restaurants.

CHEESE

During your travels two types of cheese will dominate breakfast buffets. A mild yellow cheese *(gulost)*, most likely Jarlsberg or Norvegia, is thinly sliced and eaten with bread.

The more curious selection is the peanut-butter colored block of brown cheese *(brunost)*, a tangy, sweet cheese with a fudge-like texture. Unique to Norway and technically not a cheese, brown cheese is made from the whey of cow's milk or goat's milk produced during the cheese-making process. Many variants of brown cheese exist, but the intense, caramelized taste is common to all.

Gamalost is an aged hard cheese made from soured cow's milk. It is grainy in texture, sharp and bitter in flavor, with an extremely pungent aroma.

FRUITS AND DESSERTS

Traditional Norwegian desserts such as the vanilla-cream layered *bløtkake* and the stunning conical *kransekake* are almost always home-baked and rarely found on restaurant menus. Desserts tend to utilize the fruits that grow well in cold climates, such as apples and a wide range of berries.

Strawberries are popular nationwide and can often be bought directly from farmers in stalls at gas stations and town centers. The golden cloudberry *(multe)* grows only in mountain climates and is regarded as a delicacy. They are often eaten at Christmas with whipped cream and sugar.

Sweet buns flavored with cinnamon or cardamom are a staple feature of all Norwegian cafés.

SNACKS

Spend any time traveling the country and you'll soon come across the staple Norwegian snacks of *pølser* (hot dogs), *boller* (sweet buns), and *lefser* (flatbread, often sweetened). The buns are available in a wide range of forms, from a basic bread roll *(bolle)* to ornate creations flavored with cinnamon *(kanelbolle)*. Such items sustain locals on long hiking trips and are available in abundance at roadside kiosks and gas stations and on many ferries. The budget conscious could easily make a quick lunch out of these items.

BEVERAGES

Coffee

Like the other Scandinavian countries, Norway is a nation of coffee drinkers. Strong black filter coffee is preferred to milky drinks, and a consumption of four or five cups a day is not considered unusual. When taking a guided tour or excursion that includes hot drinks, don't be surprised if black coffee is the only option.

Alcohol

The reputation of Norway having some of the highest alcohol taxes in the world is fully deserved. All alcohol is expensive, although the taxes get progressively higher with the alcohol content. Witness the rush to the duty-free store by Norwegians arriving home after an international flight for proof, along with the fact that most locals have the duty-free allowances committed to memory.

It's not just price that makes consumption of alcohol in Norway difficult. Availability can be a problem too. Outside of licensed bars and restaurants, only beer under 4.7 percent alcohol by volume can be bought in supermarkets. All other alcohol, including stronger beers, wines, and spirits, can only be purchased from the state-run off license chain, Vinmopolet. It is not possible to buy alcohol outside of bars and licensed restaurants after 8pm weekdays, 6pm Saturday, or at all on Sunday. Vinmopolet opening hours are shorter, and stores in smaller towns often close at 3pm on Saturday.

A trend for craft beer has swept the country over the past few years, with brewpubs popular in all major cities. Traditionalists prefer *akevitt* (also spelled aquavit), a spirit flavored with caraway or dill. It is a common accompaniment to fish, and is occasionally drunk together with dark beer.

Norway's accommodations vary from international chain hotels to budget campsites, and everything in between. Facilities are rarely poor, but luxury accommodations are not commonplace either. One plus point: Wi-Fi is standard across all types of accommodations, with even most budget hostels and campsites offering a free connection.

HOTELS

Hotel accommodations in cities are generally of a good standard, but expect a more basic level of service in smaller towns. In cheaper hotels, rooms advertised as double consist of two single beds pushed together. Even on double beds, two separate duvets are commonplace throughout Scandinavia. Almost all hotels will offer a Scandinavian cold breakfast buffet, more often than not included in the price.

High season for hotels is mid-June to mid-August, but curiously this tends to be when rates are at their cheapest. July is Norway's national holiday month, with most locals taking to their mountain cabin hideaways or traveling overseas for the entire month, freeing up capacity for international tourists. However, hotels in major cities and in popular areas with limited options fill up fast, so advance booking is essential during high season.

Outside of high season, availability is less of a problem, although be aware of any major festivals or conferences, which have been known to book out an entire city. Prices for swish business hotels in Oslo drop substantially at weekends. Expect to pay at least 1,000-1,500kr for an international standard hotel and 750-1,000kr for a budget hotel.

GUESTHOUSES

Somewhere between a basic hotel and a British-style bed-and-breakfast, a Norwegian guesthouse (*gjestehus* or *pensjon*) is a common sight in suburbs and smaller industrial towns. Offering comfortable, clean but basic accommodations, rooms usually share bathroom and kitchen facilities. Rooms typically run 500-750kr per night.

During high season, many householders along popular tourist routes will advertise private lodgings for rent with a simple *rom* sign by the roadside.

CABINS

Anywhere there is a shoreline you will find cabins to rent. Standards vary wildly, from a simple four-walled timber hut to a luxury Swiss-style mountain lodge.

Cabins can be rented privately, through hotel booking websites, or as part of a campsite. Typically, private cabins and those on campsites come equipped with electricity, running water, and a small kitchenette. Expect to pay 800-1,200kr for one that sleeps four, depending on location. More basic cabins without any facilities can be snapped up for around 500-700kr.

The Right to Roam

Throughout Norway, everyone has the unrestricted right to free access to the open countryside, opening up a budget accommodation option to keen campers. Known as "Allemannsretten," the legislation ensures that everyone can enjoy nature on equal terms, even within national parks.

The rules are simple: Be considerate and thoughtful, and leave no trace. The right of access applies to open countryside, which includes most shorelines, bogs, forests, mountains, and national parks. It does not apply to private fenced or cultivated land, and you must keep at least 500 feet away from private cabins or homes.

If you want to stay for more than two nights in the same place, you must ask the landowner's permission, except in the mountains or very remote areas. Picking berries, mushrooms, and wildflowers is permitted, but fires are not allowed in or near woodland between April and August. Places for emptying toilets are signposted, and doing so elsewhere is strictly prohibited.

All cabins can be rented nightly, but substantial savings are available for stays of a week or more.

Some of the pricier options have bathrooms, a number of separate bedrooms, and all the mod cons. In and around ski resorts, standards and prices rocket.

Mountain Huts

The **Norwegian Trekking Association (Den Norske Turistforening)** (DNT, tel. 40 00 18 70, www.dnt.no) maintains hundreds of small mountain cabins across their network of hiking and skiing trails. These huts are spaced out so hikers and cross-country skiers have a convenient place to stay overnight on week-long hikes. The cabins range from tiny unstaffed huts with room for two people through to hostel-style lodges with bathrooms and hot food. DNT members receive preferential rates, and no one is turned away from staffed lodges, even if you have to sleep on the floor.

HOSTELS

Most hostels *(vandrerhjem)* in Norway are only open from May to September, so you'll have to look much harder for budget accommodations if traveling in the wintertime. Dorm rooms typically sleep 4-6 with shared bathroom, kitchen, and lounge facilities. In almost all hostels, guests are required to bring their own bedding or pay a fee (50-100kr) to hire a set. The downside of hosteling in Norway is the price, typically twice what you'd pay elsewhere in Europe. A couple of uncomfortable nights in a cramped 250-350kr dorm bed may make that 600kr guesthouse seem like a steal.

More than a thousand campsites dot the Norwegian countryside, but the majority are only open from May to September, so those open in low season are in high demand. Pitches for RVs and tents are available for around 150-250kr depending on season and the facilities at the campsite. Most campsites have decent kitchen and bathroom facilities, although you should expect to pay 10kr for a shower. Many receptions double as a small kiosk selling bread and other basic groceries at vastly marked-up prices.

Health and Safety

VACCINATIONS AND GENERAL RISKS

Beyond ensuring routine vaccinations are up-to-date, no special preparations are required for travel to Norway. It's a good idea to ensure you are up to date with vaccines for measles-mumps-rubella (MMR), diphtheria-tetanus-pertussis, varicella (chickenpox), polio, and flu. Rabies is present in bats in Norway, but is not a risk to the vast majority of travelers. Only those who plan some serious hiking in remote areas should consider a rabies shot.

The biggest risks to your health in Norway are likely to be weather related. Sunburn and dehydration are possible in the summer but also when the temperatures are below freezing. Long summer days and the sun reflecting off snow in the winter can catch people unaware, so sunscreen and sunglasses are recommended. Blisters are common among inexperienced hikers, and beware of mosquito bites near water. The quality of the tap water is excellent throughout the country.

MEDICAL SERVICES

The Norwegian health care system is founded on the principles of universal access, decentralization, and free choice of provider. This means although health-care policy is handled centrally, the standard of available services can and does vary around the country. Most hospitals in Norway are public hospitals, funded and owned by the state.

Although health care is excellent, it is very expensive, and therefore comprehensive travel insurance is an absolute must. If you intend on taking part in any activities such as skiing, snowboarding, hiking, rock climbing, or motorcycling, be sure it is covered by your travel insurance, as many cheaper policies exclude many forms of outdoor activity that are popular in Norway.

EU/EEA citizens visiting Norway should obtain a free European Health Insurance Card (EHIC) before leaving their country of citizenship. The EHIC isn't a substitute for medical and travel insurance, but it entitles you to the same state-provided medical treatment as Norwegian nationals; you must pay for any treatment out of your own pocket. Reimbursement of these expenses is a matter between you and your national health insurer.

For queries on the process within Norway, contact **Helfo** (tel. 33 51 22 80, www.helfo.no). If you misplace your EHIC while in Norway, contact your country's health department for a temporary certificate. The EHIC won't cover repatriation, ongoing medical treatment, or non-urgent treatment, so comprehensive travel insurance is still highly recommended.

Bear in mind that medical facilities in remote areas are spread far apart. Search-and-rescue response will often need to be dispatched from many hundreds of miles away. If traveling through remote regions, talk to a medical professional prior to your trip and develop a contingency plan. Always be sure to have access to funds that will cover the cost of any medical treatment or potential repatriation.

CRIME

Despite the reputation given to the country by its excellent crime novelists, Norway is a safe country in which to travel. Having said that, petty theft has been on the rise in the major cities, so vigilance is still called for.

Drugs are sold openly on the streets near Oslo Central Station. Although the practice is to a certain extent tolerated, it is of course illegal.

Travel Tips

WHAT TO PACK

If you get into conversation with a local during a summer downpour, you'll inevitably hear the Norwegian saying "There's no such thing as bad weather, only bad clothing." (It's actually a lot catchier in Norwegian: *Det finnes ikke dårlig vær, bare dårlige klær.*)

To avoid being subjected to this, packing appropriate clothing is a must. This means waterproofs and plenty of layers at any time of year. Two or three thin layers is better than one thick layer, as you can easily alter your clothing depending on if and when the weather changes. Woolen underwear is an essential component to layering outside the summer. (Merino wool, while a little expensive, is suitable for most sensitive skin conditions.) Good quality hiking boots or at the very least shoes with good grip are essential if you plan to take any hikes or long walks.

If traveling in the winter, take sunglasses and sunscreen. The reflection of the bright winter sun off the snow February-April can catch many travelers by surprise. Sunburn and dehydration are possible in the summer but also when the temperatures are below freezing.

A basic first-aid kit is recommended for those who plan to hike or travel to any remote parts of the country. Be sure to include mosquito repellent, as bites can be common throughout the summer and into the fall.

Advance planning is the key to avoiding sticker-shock and saving money in one of the world's most expensive travel destinations.

Air travel and train tickets should be booked at least seven days in advance to secure the best deals. Plan your day's itinerary around mealtimes so you are in a place with multiple options when you will want to eat. Being forced to eat at the only restaurant for miles around is a sure-fire way to bust your budget.

Make the most of the generous breakfast buffets offered by hotels and most hostels. Many will allow you to make a packed lunch from the buffet for an additional 50kr, which is much less than buying lunch in a café or restaurant will cost. The quality of tap water is excellent, so invest in a refillable bottle rather than buying expensive bottled water throughout the day.

When it comes to planning your itinerary, look to the Norwegians for inspiration. On their summer vacations, Norwegians young and old tend to stay in basic accommodations, eat simple meals, and spend their time at one with nature in the mountains, fjords, and valleys. Hiking, cycling, and cross-country skiing are all outstanding ways to see the very best Norway has to offer without breaking the bank.

However, when it comes to the cost of travel in Norway, it's best to approach your trip with an open mind. To guarantee a memorable vacation, be prepared to pay for the experiences that you want, and plan to save money in other areas. Advance planning, knowing your priorities, and avoiding the constant urge to calculate the exchange rate is absolutely key to a successful trip.

BUSINESS TRAVEL

Norwegians work to live rather than live to work. Don't expect to take any business meetings on a Friday afternoon, school holidays, or the holiday month of July.

But don't let the short working hours together with the informal attitude to business dress mislead you; Norwegians make the most of their time in the office. Business lunches are short and efficient, generally involving topped open-faced sandwiches and almost never alcohol.

A national attitude toward freedom of information (an individual's tax records are a matter of public record) extends toward business, where honesty trumps a smoke-and-mirrors approach to selling.

ACCESS FOR TRAVELERS
WITH DISABILITIES

All trains are adapted for accessibility, and all stations have access ramps and lifts. Some buses, especially within cities, are equipped with ground-level entries to ease the loading of wheelchairs.

In 2014, the Council of Europe awarded the Accessibility Award to Norway for the Oslo Opera House. There is a genuine desire driven by government to improve access for people with disabilities based on equal-access policies. Most modern museums, galleries, and attractions will be equipped with ramps and lifts, while many offer special facilities for the partially sighted and hard of hearing, such as self-guided audio tours and braille information boards.

However, some historical attractions are not so well suited to accessibility because of the difficulty of adapting traditional buildings. Inquire in advance to be sure.

LGBT TRAVEL

Like their Nordic neighbors, Norwegians in general have a liberal attitude toward LGBT people. Norway was among the first countries to introduce anti-discrimination laws against LGBT people. Gays and lesbians have the same rights as heterosexuals in church weddings, adoptions, and assisted pregnancies. Many senior politicians have been openly gay or lesbian, and LGBT people are in general well integrated into society. For this reason, the gay scene is not especially large even in Oslo. The capital is home to several well-established gay bars, nightclubs, and social groups, although Bergen, Stavanger, and Trondheim also have at least one gay venue.

Oslo Pride is the country's primary LGBT festival. Held every summer, the festival provides a very visible recognition of the status of the community within Oslo, with parades, lectures, exhibitions, and political debates alongside the parties. Smaller events take place in Trondheim, Bergen, and Stavanger most years.

Skeiv Ungdom (Tollbugata 24, tel. 23 10 39 36, www.skeivungdom.no) is a nationwide youth group for LGBT people under 30. Headquartered in Oslo, the association has branches in most regions.

Although homophobic behavior can and does occur, gay and lesbian travelers should not expect to encounter any problems within Norway.

Information and Services

MONEY

Norway uses the Norwegian krone (plural kroner), commonly written as kr (after the amount) or NOK (before the amount) and often translated by enthusiastic cashiers as the Norwegian crown. Bills are in denominations of 1,000kr, 500kr, 200kr, 100kr, and 50kr. Coins are in denominations of 20kr, 10kr, 5kr, and 1kr. One Norwegian krone is made up of 100 øre, although this subdivision is rarely used now that the smallest coin in circulation is a one-krone coin. A price of 17.90 will be rounded up to 18kr in a store, although the exact amount would be charged to a debit or credit card.

The thousand separator is written as a full stop in Norwegian, with a comma used before any øre amount. For example, 1.000,50 is one-thousand kroner, fifty øre. To prevent confusion, this guide sticks to the English conventions.

The exchange rate has fluctuated wildly between 5.5kr and 8.9kr per US$1 over the past five years. At the time of writing, US$1 bought about 8.1kr.

Changing money can be troublesome, as many bank branches no longer carry cash, and rates on offer at exchange bureaus leave a lot to be desired. The best rates can usually be obtained by simply withdrawing cash from an ATM, but be aware of what your own bank will charge you for this service. Many banks have ATMs inside a vestibule that is open outside of regular banking hours.

Debit and credit cards are the primary form of payment in almost all Norwegian stores, regardless of the amount. Digital solutions are rapidly taking over from cash, so much so that cash is expected to be phased out from everyday transactions in the coming years. It's a good idea nonetheless to keep some cash on you at all times, as some of the cheaper card readers only accept Norwegian debit cards. For all ferries and the vast majority of tourist attractions, international credit cards will work fine.

Tipping

Tipping is not necessary in restaurants because all staff are paid a fair wage. Rounding up the bill is considered a compliment on the service. However, don't be surprised to see extra enthusiasm from your waiter or waitress when they realize you are a foreigner. North Americans are especially well looked after given their reputation for tipping well.

Taxes

If you buy goods priced more than 315kr from stores that display the blue Tax Free logo, you're entitled to a refund of the 25 percent MVA, the Norwegian equivalent of a sales tax that is added to the price of most goods and services. At the point of sale, you must complete a form, which you then present at your point of departure along with the goods to claim your refund. Tourist information offices stock an information leaflet detailing the process, as do all shops displaying the logo.

COMMUNICATIONS
Telephone

The country code for Norway is 47. Norwegian phone numbers are eight digits long, and there are no area codes. To call a number from within the country, you just dial the eight digits. (Some information services and taxi providers use special shortened five-digit numbers that start with 0; in these cases, you just dial the five digits.) To call Norway from abroad, dial the international access code plus 47 followed by the five- or eight-digit number.

The directory inquiry service at **Gule Sider** (www.gulesider.no) will provide the phone numbers of the majority of businesses and individuals and also allow you to find the owner of a phone number.

MOBILE PHONES

Roaming prices across the European Economic Area (EEA) were slashed in 2016, meaning that most citizens of EEA countries can use their mobile phones in Norway as if they were in their home country; check with your carrier for confirmation and any exceptions. For others, prepaid SIM cards can be purchased in convenience stores and in kiosks in all airports and public transport hubs. **Telenor** (www.telenor.no) and **Telia** (www.telia.no) are the two biggest carriers in Norway and offer cards for 100kr and 200kr suitable for calls and text messages, and up to 500kr for data. Other options include **Chess** (www.chess.no) and **Lycamobile** (www.lyca-mobile.no).

Internet Access

Wireless Internet connectivity is commonplace in Norwegian hotels, shopping centers, and cafés. Most require a simple login procedure with a password that can be obtained from reception or on purchase of an item.

TIME ZONE

All of Norway observes Central European Time (CET), which is one hour ahead of Greenwich Mean Time (GMT) and six hours ahead of the U.S. Eastern time zone. Daylight Saving Time is observed but the exact dates can differ by a week or two from the United States, so double-check if traveling in the spring or fall.

WEIGHTS AND MEASURES

Norway uses the metric system. All road signs are in kilometers and all weights are given in kilograms/grams. Beer is served in liters, with 0.4 and 0.6 used commonly used to indicate 400 ml (small) and 600 ml (large) respectively.

Standard voltage in Norway is 230 V. The power sockets take the rounded two-prong Type F plugs, which are common across much of mainland Europe. Power adapters are available from airports, major train stations, and **Clas Ohlson** (www.clasohlson.com) and **Lefdal** (www.lefdal.com) stores across the country.

Resources

Glossary

In Norwegian (and unlike in English), descriptive words such as lake *(vann, vannet, vatnet)*, mountain *(fjell)*, waterfall *(foss, fossen)*, and so on are incorporated into the place name. This is handy information to know when you are unsure what a place name might mean.

akevitt: a traditional Scandinavian distilled spirit spiced with caraway or dill; also known as aquavit

bacalao: dried and salted cod, typically cooked in a tomato-based sauce; not to be confused with the Spanish word *bacalao* (fresh cod)

bidos: slow-cooked reindeer stew, a traditional Sami dish

bløtkake: a layer cake of vanilla sponge and cream, often decorated with strawberries

brunost: brown cheese, a sweet dairy product and one of Norway's most iconic foods

by: city or town, all places from Oslo down to all but the smallest villages

dal: valley

damer: ladies; may be displayed on a bathroom door as simply "D"

ferge: ferry

fjell: mountain

foss, fossen: waterfall

fylke: county; Norway is split into 19 counties, although that number is set to decrease in the coming years as several counties merge (road numbers sometimes change across county borders)

gamalost/gammelost: extremely strong, firm, sour cheese; hard to find outside Norway

gate: street

gjestehus: guesthouse

gulost: any variety of mild, yellow cheese

herrer: gentlemen; may be displayed on a bathroom door as simply "H"

hval: whale

hytte: cabin

jolk: a traditional Sami folk song

kjøttboller: meatballs

kjøttkaker: larger meatballs (but smaller than a burger patty)

kommune: municipality

kransekake: an eye-catching traditional celebratory cake, made up of donut-like rings piled into a pyramid

kvæfjordkake: a cake of meringue, almond, and vanilla cream

lavvu: a traditional large Sami tent

lefse/lefser: a soft flatbread of varying thickness, commonly served with butter, sugar, and/or cinnamon

lege: doctor

legevakt: emergency room; sometimes, but not always, colocated at a hospital

lutefisk: dried cod treated with lye, a Norwegian speciality of acquired taste

matpakke: a packed lunch, typically consisting of sandwiches

pensjon: guesthouse, bed-and-breakfast

pinnekjøtt: dried and salted lamb

plass: place, typically a public square

pølser: hot dog sausages, typically served in buns or a tortilla-like wrap

risgrøt: rice porridge, often served at Christmas

rom: room

rorbuer: traditional fisherman's cabin, often now used as vacation cabins

sentrum: downtown

stengt: closed

stranda: beach

sykehus: hospital

tannlege: dentist

torsk: cod

ungdom: youth

vandrerhjem: hostel

vann, vannet, vatnet: lake

ABBREVIATIONS

Ca: often precedes a time on a live information board at public transit stops; it indicates an approximate time, usually the time listed on the timetable when live information is unavailable

Fv: fylkesvei (county road)

kr: kroner, the currency of Norway, which translates as "crowns"; also occasionally written before the number as NOK (Norwegian kroner)

Mvh: med vennlig hilsen (with kind regards); often used as a shorthand way of signing off a letter or email

Rv: riksvei (national road)

English is spoken and understood throughout Norway by all but the oldest generation. A little Norwegian goes a long way toward getting a smile, but the person will almost certainly respond to you in English. Don't take offense, as Norwegians absolutely love to practice their English with native speakers.

PRONUNCIATION

Regional dialects are strong throughout Norway, so don't be dismayed if you cannot understand the locals, particularly in Bergen and the rural regions surrounding the fjords. The biggest differences tend to be with pronunciation of prepositions, which can make understanding even basic sentences difficult for beginners.

Almost all Norwegian lessons teach the standard Eastern Norwegian dialect, also known as the Oslo dialect. Most Norwegian words place the emphasis on the first syllable, which results in the sing-song melody the language is known for.

Vowels

Each vowel can be either long or short. As a general rule, a vowel is long if it followed by one consonant and short if it is followed by two. This distinguishes *tak* (roof) from *takk* (thanks). Norwegian has three extra vowels at the end of the alphabet: æ, ø, and å. Although at first confusing, the sounds all exist in English.

a   resembles the a in "tar"
e   resembles the e in "left"
i   resembles the ee in "teeth"
o   resembles the o in "lord" or the oo in "soon" when long
u   resembles the oo in "foot"
y   English speakers have trouble with this vowel; a good approximation is to make an "ee" sound but with pursed lips
æ   resembles the a in "hat"
ø   resembles the u in "burn"
å   resembles the o in "lord"

Consonants

The letters c, q, w, x, and z are rare and only tend to be used in foreign loan words. Notable differences in pronunciation include:

g   like the hard English g, except when used before i or j when it resembles the y in "yes"; also, a g is always silent at the end of a word
j   resembles the y in "yes"
k   like the hard English k, except when used before I or j, when it resembles the soft ch in "loch"
r   a very soft sound, like the "r" in "feather"; some dialects roll the r as in Spanish

BASIC EXPRESSIONS

Norwegian is a simple direct language and can appear abrupt when translated. For example, there is no direct equivalent for please, and using the nearest equivalent, *vær så snill*, is only required in the most formal of scenarios. You can add *takk* (thank you) on to the end of a request to convey politeness. To start a conversation with a Norwegian, a simple *Hei! (hay)* (Hi!) or *Unnskyld? (un-shull)* (Excuse me?)) is all that is required.

Hello. *Hallo.*

Hi. *Hei.*

Good morning. *God morgen.*

How are you? *Hvordan går det?*

I'm fine, thank you. *Jeg har det bra, takk.*

Thank you. *Takk.*

Thank you very much. *Tusen takk.*

You're welcome. *Vær så god.*

No problem. *Bare hyggelig.*

Good-bye. *Ha det bra.*

yes *ja*

no *nei*

I don't know. *Jeg vet ikke.*

Just a moment. *Ett øyeblikk.*

Excuse me? *Unnskyld?*

Sorry. *Beklager.*

What is your name? *Hva heter du?*

My name is . . . *Jeg heter . . .*

Pleased to meet you. *Hyggelig å treffe deg.*

Do you speak English? *Snakker du engelsk?*

I don't understand Norwegian. *Jeg forstår ikke norsk.*

Where is the bathroom? *Hvor er toalettet?*

Ladies *Damer*

Gentlemen *Herrer*

TERMS OF ADDRESS

Norwegians often address people using just their surname or simply saying *du* (you).

I *Jeg*

you *du/dere* (singular/plural)

he *han*

she *hun*

we *vi*

they *de*

man *mann*

woman *kvinne*

boy *gutt*

girl *jente*

husband *ektemann*

wife *kone*
friend *venn*
son *sønn*
daughter *datter*
brother *bror*
sister *søster*
father *far*
mother *mor*
grandfather *bestefar*
grandmother *bestemor*

TRANSPORTATION

car *bil*
bus *buss*
train *tog*
boat *båt*
plane *fly*
airport bus *flybuss*
the border *grensen*
customs *toll*
immigration *innvandring*
passport *pass*
insurance *forsikring*
driver's license *førerkort*
Where is . . . ? *Hvor er . . . ?*
How far is it to . . . ? *Jeg vet ikke . . . ?*
(the) bus station *busstasjon(en), bussterminal(en)*
(the) train station *jernbanestasjon(en)*
(the) ferry port *fergelei(et), fergekai(en)*
(the) airport *flyplass(en)*
downtown *sentrum*
Where is the train/bus/ferry to . . . ? *Hvor finner jeg toget/bussen/fergen til . . . ?*
Does this stop at . . . ? *Stopper denne på . . . ?*
How much is a ticket to . . . ? *Hva koster en billett til . . . ?*
I want to go to . . . *Jeg skal til . . .*
one-way *en vei*
round-trip *tur/retur* (literally, trip/return)
canceled *kansellert, avlyst*
delayed *forsinket*
north *nord*
south *sør, syd*
east *øst*
west *vest*
left *venstre*
right *høyre*

ACCOMMODATIONS

hotel *hotell*
youth hostel *vandrerhjem*
campsite *camping*
cabin *hytte*
guesthouse *gjestehus/pensjon*
apartment *leilighet*
room *rom*
bathroom *bad*
balcony *balkong*
Is there a single/double room? *Finnes det et enkeltrom/dobbelrom?*
How much does it cost per night? *Hva koster det per natt?*
Is breakfast included? *Er frokost inkludert?*

FOOD

When ordering food, it is common to simply state the specific item with no "Can I have …" preceding it. Another option is to precede the item with *Jeg tar…*, which literally means "I'll take …" With no direct equivalent for please, use *takk* (thanks) after the order to convey politeness.

breakfast *frokost*
lunch *lunsj*
dinner *middag*
a table for two *et bord til to*
menu *meny*
What does it include? *Hva inkluderer det?*
I am allergic to … *Jeg er allergisk mot …*
I don't eat meat. *Jeg spiser ikke kjøtt.*
Is there a menu in English? *Finnes det en meny på engelsk?*
fork *gaffel*
knife *kniv*
spoon *skje*
the check *regningen*
a glass of water *et glass vann*
a glass of wine *et glass vin*
beer *øl*
coffee *kaffe*
juice *jus*
red wine *rødvin*
soft drink *brus*
tea *te*
white wine *hvitvin*
with/without milk *med/uten melk*
with/without cream *med/uten krem*
with/without sugar *med/uten suker*
meat *kjøtt*
fish *fisk*

seafood *sjømat*
beef *oksekjøtt, storfekjøtt*
chicken *kylling*
cod *torsk*
dried cod *tørrfisk*
dried cod (salted) *klippfisk*
duck *and*
halibut *kveite*
herring *sild*
lamb *lam*
mackerel *makrell*
pork *svinekjøtt*
reindeer *reinsdyr*
salmon *laks*
shellfish *skalldyr*
shrimp *reker*
trout *ørret*
whale *hval*
fruit *frukt*
vegetables *grønnsaker*
apple *eple*
banana *banan*
beans *bønner*
blueberry *blåbær*
carrot *gulrot*
cloudberry *multe*
corn *korn/mais*
orange *appelsin*
pineapple *ananas*
potato *potet*
raspberry *bringebær*
strawberry *jordbær*
tomato *tomat*
nuts *nøtter*
wheat *hvete*
dairy products *melkeprodukter*
butter *smør*
cheese *ost*
ice cream *is*
milk *melk*
pepper *pepper*
salt *salt*

SHOPPING
I'm looking for ... *Jeg letter etter ...*
How much does it cost? *Hva koster det?*

money *penger*
ATM *minibank*
credit card *kredittkort*
shopping mall *kjøpesenter*

HEALTH

Can you help me? *Kan du hjelpe meg?*
I am ill. *Jeg er syk.*
I need a doctor. *Jeg trenger en lege.*
pharmacy *apotek*
hospital *sykehus*
doctor *lege*
dentist *tannlege*
emergency room *legevakt*
pain *smerte*
fever *feber*
nausea *kvalme*
vomiting *oppkast*

NUMBERS

zero *null*
one *en, ett*
two *to*
three *tre*
four *fire*
five *fem*
six *seks*
seven *sju, syv*
eight *åtte*
nine *ni*
10 *ti*
11 *elleve*
12 *tolv*
13 *tretten*
14 *fjorten*
15 *femten*
16 *seksten*
17 *sytten*
18 *atten*
19 *nitten*
20 *tjue, tyve*
30 *tretti*
40 *førti*
50 *femti*
60 *seksti*
70 *sytti*

80 *åtti*
90 *nitti*
100 *(ett) hundre*
101 *(ett) hundre og en*
200 *to hundre*
500 *fem hundre*
1,000 *(ett) tusen*
2,000 *to tusen*
1,000,000 *en million*
half *halv*
quarter *kvart*
less *mindre*
more *mer*

TIME

Time is usually written using the 24-hour clock, so supermarket opening hours of 8-20 mean 8am-8pm. Stores often put Saturday hours in parentheses, with the assumption it will be closed on Sunday: e.g., 8-20 (10-16).

When time is spoken, it's common to use the 12-hour clock. The biggest difference is how half-hours are treated. *Halv fire* translates as "half to four" not "half past four" as you would first expect. If in doubt, always ask for written confirmation of times. It's also a good idea never to say "half four" to a Norwegian when you mean 4:30, as it could well be misunderstood.

What time is it? *Hva er klokka?*
It's one o'clock. *Klokka er ett.*
It's five past one. *Klokka er fem over ett.*
It's quarter past eight. *Klokka er kvart over åtte.*
It's 3:35. *Klokka er fem over halv fire.*
noon *middagstid*
midnight *midnatt*
morning *morgen*
afternoon *ettermiddag*
evening *kveld*
night *natt*
yesterday *i går*
today *i dag*
tomorrow *i morgen*
an hour *en time*
a day *en dag*
a week *en uke*
a month *en måned*
a year *et år*

DAYS, MONTHS, AND SEASONS

Days, months, and seasons are always written in lowercase. A common way to write the date is the number followed by a dot followed by the first three letters of the month: e.g., 4.jul for July 4.

Monday *mandag*
Tuesday *tirsdag*
Wednesday *onsdag*
Thursday *torsdag*
Friday *fredag*
Saturday *lørdag*
Sunday *søndag*
January *januar*
February *februar*
March *mars*
April *april*
May *mai*
June *juni*
July *juli*
August *august*
September *september*
October *oktober*
November *november*
December *desember*
spring *vår*
summer *sommer*
autumn *høst*
winter *vinter*

Suggested Reading

HISTORY

Hunt, Vincent. *Fire and Ice: The Nazis' Scorched Earth Campaign in Norway.* The History Press, 2014. Norway's grim World War II history is told in thousands of Norwegian language books, but previously little existed in English. British journalist Vincent Hunt traveled across Arctic Norway to uncover the human tales behind the devastation of Finnmark at the end of the war.

Roesdahl, Else. *The Vikings.* Penguin, 1998. Hundreds of books exist profiling the most famous period of Nordic history, but this one can be considered the gold standard. Roesdahl gives the Scandinavian perspective on the art, customs, and daily life of the Viking people, blowing wide open their reputation as a band of savage explorers.

Holt, Anne. *1222*. Scribner, 2012. As the former Norwegian Minister of Justice, Holt brings an air of realism to her detective novels. A classic locked-room mystery, *1222* is set in an atmospheric snowed-in mountain hotel following a train crash on the Oslo to Bergen railway.

MacLean, Alistair. *Bear Island*. Harper, 2009 reissue. A converted fishing trawler carries a production crew across the Barents Sea for some on-location filming, but the script is known only to the producer and screen-writer. On the way to remote Bear Island, members of the crew begin to die under mysterious circumstances. It seems that nearly everyone in the crew had secrets and were not who they claimed to be.

Nesbø, Jo. *The Redbreast*. Harper Perennial, 2008. The former soccer player, financial analyst, and rock star turned his hand to crime novels in 1997 and hasn't looked back since. His series following fictional Oslo sleuth Harry Hole investigating a series of gruesome murders is a worldwide smash. *The Redbreast* is the best introduction and won't spoil the earlier books.

LITERATURE

Gaader, Jostein. *Sophie's World*. Weidenfeld & Nicolson, 1994. One of the most globally successful Norwegian novels, *Sophie's World* is a long, complex tale of teenage Sophie Amundsen, who begins to learn philosophy under the guidance of a middle-aged professor. As Sophie begins to question the world in which she lives, the story takes an unlikely twist. A little heavy on the philosophy it may be, but it's key to developing the story.

Jacobsen, Roy. *Child Wonder*. Graywolf Press, 2011. In this uplifting com-ing-of-age novel set in 1960s Oslo, eight-year-old Finn lives with his mother, and they just about make ends meet in a working-class suburb. Soon Finn experiences dramatic change as a lodger arrives, followed by a younger sister whom he never knew existed. An intricately worked story, rich in detail and a beautiful exploration of an adult world through the mind of a child.

Kirkwood, Thomas, and Geir Finne. *The Svalbard Passage*. CreateSpace, 2011. Co-written by Norwegian and American authors, this Cold War thriller has a familiar premise—the United States and the United Soviet Socialist Republic on the verge of nuclear war—but with an unfamiliar setting: the Norwegian Arctic territory of Svalbard. Not the most dra-matic of thrillers, yet the dramatic descriptions of Svalbard will draw you into the story.

Knausgård, Karl Ove. *A Death in the Family.* Farrar, Straus, and Giroux, 2013. The first in the *My Struggle* autobiographical series that captivated Norwegian readers for years before the books made their international breakthrough, this honest window exposes the fragility of the teenage mind while providing a frank and critical look at those who influenced the author's early years. Odds are you'll want to read the remaining five parts in this epic series.

SOCIETY AND CULTURE

Booth, Michael. *The Almost Nearly Perfect People: The Truth About the Nordic Miracle.* Picador, 2015. Loved and criticized in equal measure, British journalist Booth's study of the Nordic people is skewed toward his perceptions of his adopted homeland Denmark, but it contains some interesting observations on Norwegians, in particular their attitude toward their Swedish and Danish siblings.

Mytting, Lars. *Norwegian Wood: Chopping, Stacking and Drying Wood the Scandinavian Way.* MacLehose Press, 2015. Surely one of the most unlikely nonfiction successes ever written, this handbook on the Norwegian relationship with the forest has sold over half a million copies worldwide. Mytting has distilled the chopping, storing, drying, and burning wisdom of professionals and enthusiasts into this truly Scandinavian tome. You'll never look at your firewood in the same way again.

Seierstad, Anne. *One of Us: The Story of Anders Breivik and the Massacre in Norway.* Virago, 2015. When the peaceful Utøya island was scarred forever in 2011, Norwegians were taken aback that the atrocity had been committed by one of their own. Beginning with a powerful narrative from the island, Norwegian journalist Seierstad proceeds to provide a meticulously researched, honest yet compassionate account of the tragedy, as well as the background of the man behind it.

FOOD

Love, Whitney. *Thanks for the Food: The Culinary Adventures of an American in Norway.* Digital Word Norway, 2014. An American expat living in Stavanger, Love turned her popular food blog into a recipe book that combines the traditional national dishes with a modern twist on classic ingredients. She also shares her tips for travelers wanting to make the most of their visits to Norway's famous agricultural, fishing, and dairy regions.

Thorud, Richard A. *Aunt Hildur's Excellent Norwegian Recipes.* Elliot House, 2013. This very small book is reminiscent of the recipes Norwegian grandmothers would have passed around at church decades ago. It's worth it for the traditional methods of making *lefse* and *kransekake* without lots of fancy, modern equipment.

Brett, Jan. *Trouble with Trolls*. G.P. Putnam's Sons, 2016 reissue. This beautifully illustrated 32-page hardback is the perfect way to get younger children excited about a visit to Norway. The story follows Treva and her dog Tuffi as they set out to climb Mount Baldy. But the mountain is inhabited by a family of trolls who wish for a dog. Every page details a new challenge for Treva and Tuffi as they bid to outwit the trolls.

Preus, Margi. *Shadow on the Mountain*. Amulet Books, 2012. Written by a Minnesota native, this novel captures the atmosphere and danger of living in Norway during World War II. Loosely based on real events, the part spy thriller part coming-of-age tale follows teenager Epsen as he is swept up in the resistance movement, first by delivering underground newsletters and eventually becoming a spy.

Internet Resources

HIKING

Norwegian Trekking Association (Den Norske Turistforening)
www.dnt.no
Your starting point for planning a hiking trip, DNT provides a wealth of information about the vast network of hiking trails, cross-country skiing routes, and cabins across the country.

UT
www.ut.no
This site offers detailed maps and instructions for hiking trails across the country, from beginner to week-long expeditions. Large maps can be printed or downloaded to a GPS device. It's only available in Norwegian but useful regardless.

NEWS AND MEDIA

Aftenposten
www.aftenposten.no
Aftenposten is a national daily newspaper with a particular focus on Oslo. Occasionally, major breaking news is published in English.

The Local
www.thelocal.no
The Local is the most frequently updated English-language news source.

NRK

www.nrk.no

State broadcaster NRK runs several TV channels, a breaking news website, a radio station, and a vast podcast network. Occasionally, major breaking news is published in English.

SOCIETY

A Frog in the Fjord

www.afroginthefjord.com

The funniest website about Norway, this expat blog written by a French lady living in Oslo since 2010 has been syndicated and translated into Norwegian by major newspapers.

Life in Norway

www.lifeinnorway.net

Expats from all over the world who have made Norway their home contribute to this insider look on Norwegian culture and society.

TRAVEL INFORMATION

Avinor

www.avinor.no

Almost all Norwegian airports are run by state-owned Avinor, whose website provides excellent live departure and arrivals information plus a detailed rundown of facilities available at each airport, all fully translated into English. Their excellent **Avinor Flights** app (download link on website) is a useful way to access the same live information on the move.

Norwegian Public Roads Administration (Statens Vegvesen)

www.vegvesen.no

The place to go for all driving-related information. Of particular interest to travelers is the list of toll roads and the current status of road closures.

Visit Norway

www.visitnorway.com

The country's official travel guide is maintained by Innovation Norway, a body given the responsibility to promote Norway as an attractive travel destination by the Ministry of Trade, Industry, and Fisheries.

Norway Traveller

www.norwaytraveller.com

Destination guides and travel blog about visiting Norway for international tourists. Includes advice on hunting for the northern lights, skiing in Norway, and enjoying the best of Norway on a budget.

Yr

www.yr.no

A joint venture between state broadcaster NRK and the Norwegian Meteorological Institute, Yr provides excellent hyperlocal weather forecasts, including rain and wind. Download the app for weather on the move.

INDEX

List of Maps

Front Map

Oslo